VALUES
THAT LAST

BOOKS BY THE SAME AUTHOR

VALUES
THAT LAST

CLOVIS G. CHAPPELL

ABINGDON PRESS

NEW YORK ● NASHVILLE

VALUES THAT LAST

Copyright 1939 by Whitmore & Smith

Library of Congress Catalog Card Number: 39-21399

PRINTED AND BOUND AT NASHVILLE,
TENNESSEE, UNITED STATES OF AMERICA

TO THE MEMBERS OF ST. LUKE'S CHURCH, WHOSE PRAYERFUL HELP AND CO-OPERATION MADE THESE SERMONS POSSIBLE, THIS VOLUME IS AFFECTIONATELY DEDICATED.

CONTENTS

CONTENTS

7

I

THE UNFINISHED SERMON

> *"And as Paul reasoned of right-*
> *eousness, temperance, and judg-*
> *ment to come, Felix trembled, and*
> *answered, Go thy way for this time;*
> *when I have a convenient season, I*
> *will call for thee."*

ACTS 24:25

I

FELIX WAS A BLACK SHEEP. HE WAS SO VERY black that he was conspicuous, even in a day when this color was more prevalent among politicians than it is today. Born a slave, Felix had managed in some way to win his freedom. Not only so, but by dint of considerable ability and of far more rascality he had worked his way up to a position of power. But in spite of his lofty position, he was still a moral pigmy. Whatever sovereignty he had was on the outside of him. Within, he was still in bondage. Tacitus tells us that he ruled in the spirit of a slave with all cruelty and lust. He was, therefore, the very last man that we expected to find looking toward the heights in seeming quest of a better life.

9

But even this hardened man had one big moment that was full of promise. As this scene opens, we are greeted by a joyous surprise. We find Felix at church. This does not mean that he has gone out to God's house, but that he has brought God's messenger to himself. He has sent for Paul to hear him concerning his faith in Christ. Sad to say, Felix is at this service with a heavy handicap. Beside him is a woman who is not his wife. She is the wife of another. This woman is a Jewess by the name of Drusilla. She has had a better opportunity religiously than Felix, but she has made little of it. She is as fair outwardly as she is rotten inwardly, which means that she is a very beautiful woman. But in spite of this sordid relationship, in spite of his soiled past and his dirty present, Felix has come to church. He has done so of his own free will. That in itself gives us hope.

Why, I wonder, did this renegade attend this service? What has brought him to church?

1. He may have been prompted by mere curiosity. He knew something of Paul. He had met him face to face. Only yesterday he had presided at a brief court session where Paul was at once the prisoner at the bar and the attorney for the defense. The preacher had handled his case with such consummate skill as to win the grudging admiration of Felix. There was no mistaking the fact that this prisoner was no ordinary man. Even his enemies had to confess that he had turned

the world upside down. Perhaps Felix wanted to see his amazing prisoner at closer range. Therefore, he sent for him and sat under his ministry, but with no higher motive than idle curiosity.

2. Felix may have sent for Paul because he was bored. When Felix had won his freedom, he chose a name for himself that signifies "happy." But Mr. Happy was not in reality happy at all. He was tired, bored, fed up. Though he had given reign to every lust, life had lost its tang. Felix was greatly in need of a new thrill. There is pleasure in sin, of course, but it soon grows stale. This is because sin has nothing new up its sleeve. It has been well said that if a rake from Babylon were to come back and visit our night life, he would stifle a yawn and say, "I saw all this in Babylon more than twenty-five centuries ago." Maybe Felix attended this service because he was bored.

3. Felix may have been present because of a desire for material gain. Luke tells us that, when later on, he sent for Paul, it was in the hope that Paul would give him a bribe for setting him free. If Felix was thus trying to capitalize on his church attendance, he would not be in a class entirely by himself. There have been those throughout the centuries who have sought to use the church. Some have made it a smoke screen behind which to hide their rascality. Others have attended because they had something to sell, or were eager to advance their ambitions. I am quite certain that there are comparatively few of these. Yet, there

are some, and Felix may have been of this number He may have listened to Paul with no higher motives than those that prompt a gambler to take part in a game of chance.

4. But suppose we give this royal rascal the benefit of the doubt. Suppose we assume that he attended this service because he really had a hungry heart. Suppose that we concede that there was still growing in the fetid soil of his soul, like a white flower, a longing for a better life. This is not an unreasonable assumption. Such longings have stirred, times without number, in the hearts of men just as hopeless and hard as was Felix. What faithful minister has not spoken with fear and trembling to some man regarded as hopeless, to find himself answered, not by insults as he feared, but by eager longing and penitential tears? It may be, therefore, that Felix was at church, even as you and I, because he was possessed of an insatiable hunger for God.

But after all, while the motives of Felix in attending this service are of importance, they are not of supreme importance. The proprietor of a certain department store has this motto pasted behind the counter, where it can be seen only by his salesmen: "It is not what the customer comes in after, but what he goes out with, that matters." So it is with church attendance. Many that have come to scoff have remained to pray. This is Paul's hope as he faces Felix.

THE UNFINISHED SERMON

II

What did Paul have to say to this sinner and his paramour? Suppose we slip in and share the pew of Felix and Drusilla. Do not let the suggestion shock you. They are sinners, I know, but so are we. The difference between us is one of degree rather than of kind. Therefore, what Paul said to them he is saying to you and me. Let us then, along with them, take our place at the feet of this messenger of God.

It is a favorite comment that Paul in his message to these desperate sinners has nothing to say about the love of God. One commentator remarks that we have heard of the love of God till some of us have grown love-sick. But it is my conviction that Paul's sermon is motivated and shot through with love. Love is the very warp and woof of it. I am sure of this because of the effect it had upon the hearer. It is true that love is not mentioned in the fragment of the sermon that we have, but bear in mind that Paul did not get to finish his sermon. The physician had hardly finished diagnosing the disease before the patient walked out on him. Felix adjourned the meeting. He left the service before the benediction. Therefore we have only a part of Paul's sermon, that part that was meant to search this man's soul. Look at it!

1. Paul reasoned of righteousness. I like that word "reasoned." He did not rant. He did not merely beat the air. He did not go off in sentimental gush. He reasoned. He spoke of the sanity, the thoroughgoing

13

common sense, of being right and of doing right. He showed that sin is insanity. In doing so he was taking his cue from his Master. Jesus once told the story of a graceless laddie that left a home of love and plenty to starve in a hog pen. He explained the boy's conduct, not by saying that he was too clear-headed to stay at home. He said rather that he was beside himself. The stupidity, the madness, of the wrongdoer is seen in the fact that such a one flings himself against the forces of the universe. The very stars in their courses fight against him.

The one supremely sane something, on the other hand, is righteousness. A righteous God can give his full sanction to a righteous man, and to none other. He can put all his infinite resources at his disposal. Righteousness, therefore, is fundamental. There is no really sane living without it. Surely there is no vital Christianity without it. No amount of work, no amount of religiosity, nothing, is a substitute for right living.

When the early apostles were arrested and commanded to leave off their preaching, they gave this heroic answer, "Whether it be right in the sight of God to hearken unto you more than unto God, judge ye." What is the meaning of this answer? This is what they are saying: "Our first purpose is not to save our own skins. It is not to win applause. It is not to have an easy time. Our one purpose is to do the right as God gives us to see the right." That is to be our one pur-

pose. Absolutely nothing can take the place of that.
The call of this hour and of every hour is for righteousness, rightness. We need to be right with God and
right with man. We need to be right in all our relationships, national and international. We need rightness between capital and labor, rightness in public
office, rightness in the home. We need to handle the
tools of our daily trade as religiously as we pray.
Naturally, therefore, Paul reasoned of righteousness.

2. Paul reasoned of temperance—self-mastery, self-
control. He spoke of temperance to a man who was
dressing his soul in chains. He spoke of self-control
to one who had put the reins of his life into the foul
hands of his lusts. He spoke of self-mastery to one
whose passions and appetites were bullying him and
scourging him and bringing him to heel like a common
cur. He tried to make Felix see something of the
tragedy of changing a habitation meant for the Holy
Spirit into a pigsty. He tried to bring him to the
realization that self-reverence, self-knowledge, self-
control, these three alone, lead to sovereign power. He
spoke home to this man's need. He reasoned of temperance.

3. Paul reasoned of judgment to come. Ministers
of yesterday used to preach quite a bit about judgment.
But it has been a long time, I dare say, since you
heard a sermon on this subject. Yet the Bible speaks
of judgment again and again. And there is always
sanity in what it says. I find it easy to believe in a

judgment to come because of the judgments of the past and of the present. Judgment is something that is taking place all of the time. God is constantly coming in judgment upon nations and upon individuals. Where are the bloody despotisms that once flourished upon the banks of the Euphrates and the Tigris? Where is mighty Rome with her far-flung tyrannies? God came in judgment upon them and said, "Depart ye cursed," and they passed away. Where is the Europe that went mad in its lust for power before the World War? God came in judgment upon it, and it slipped into an abysm of blood and tears. What of the Europe that was made by a treaty born of hate and revenge? That Europe is experiencing the judgment of God at this moment, and is therefore hanging upon the verge of the abyss.

As God judges the world, even so he judges the individual. This he does in the very nature of things. Every time I stand at the forks of the road and take the lower instead of the higher, I undergo judgment. This is my sentence: I find it easier, ever after, to take the lower road and harder to take the higher. When I face the light and refuse to see it, I am judged in that I lose, in some measure, my capacity to see. When I hear the truth and refuse to respond to it, my sentence is that I become a little more dull of hearing. When my heart is stirred by the wooing of the Spirit and I refuse to yield, my sentence is that I lose my sensitiveness. Paul reasoned of righteousness, of temperance, and of judgment.

III

What effect did this sermon have on Felix? Here is the way I should have expected this story to read:

"As Paul reasoned of righteousness and temperance and judgment to come, Felix sneered. Felix laughed outright in gleeful scorn. 'You are trying to frighten me,' he chuckled. 'Don't you know that I have run past such childish rubbish long ago? Don't you realize that I am smart enough to know that all your commandments were made by men to frighten timid souls into being good? Don't make me laugh!'" But this was not his reaction.

No more did Felix get angry. When Paul began to talk about being right to a man who knew he was wrong, when he spoke of self-mastery to one whose lusts had him bridled and saddled, the preacher was getting fairly personal. In the language of the farm, "he was plowing close to the corn." It would have been very natural for this royal sinner to have resented such plain preaching. He might easily have glared at the Apostle and said, "You are my prisoner. You can't talk to me like that. Such bold words are likely to cause you to land in a dungeon." But renegade that he was, he did not get angry.

What then, I repeat, was the effect of Paul's sermon? "As Paul reasoned of righteousness, temperance, and judgment to come, Felix trembled." How amazing! As I watched him, I saw him clinch his fists till his knuckles grew white, and his nails bit into the palms of his hands. I saw the big beads of perspiration break out on his face. I saw him shake like a man in the grip of a heavy chill. Then with a cry that was half a sob he shouted, "It's enough, Paul. I know you are right. I know that it is reasonable that a man should be right. I know I ought to be master of myself instead of the slave of myself. I know it is reasonable to expect judgment. You are right. But I have heard enough. Go thy way for this time. It is not convenient for me to respond to your message today. When I have a moment," as Moffatt translates it, "I will call for you."

Thus Felix interrupted the Apostle just as he was reaching the climax of his sermon. Had he waited a moment Paul would have told him of a Christ that was able to make him right at the center of his being. He would have told him that, just as leperous Naaman's flesh came back to him like the flesh of a little child, so he could be made anew. Had he only listened a little longer, Paul would have told him of One that could set him free, in whose fellowship he need never come into judgment. But the sermon was never finished. Felix adjourned the meeting and left, in the truest possible sense, without the benediction. In later days he sent for Paul again and again. But he never trembled any more. For two whole years he lived in the same house with this great saint, but that privilege was worth no more to Felix than if Paul had been a mummy. Felix had missed that high tide of the Spirit, that, taken at the flood, would have led him to life eternal.

IV

Why did Felix fail? Why did he face his big moment only to throw it away?

He did not fail because of ignorance. He could not blame his failure on the fact that he did not understand Paul. He could not claim that the whole business was too deep for one like himself who had no head for religion. He understood far too clearly for his comfort. Therefore, he could no more plead ignorance than you and I. We confess that ours is a day of moral confusion. Many of us have so lost our skyline that we cannot tell where the earth leaves off and the heavens begin. At times we are glad to lay blame for our wrong choices on this confusion. But the truth is the other way around. It is not so much that our moral confusion has led to wrong choices as that our wrong choices have led to moral confusion. Our trouble, as that of Felix, is not that we know too little; it is rather that we fail to live up to what we actually know.

No more did Felix fail because his clay soul was so shattered as to be beyond remaking. That is never the case. He failed because he refused to give God a chance. God, through his prophet, woke him up; but that was all that even God could do. He wakes us, but we must do the getting up ourselves. When I was a schoolboy I used to get up by an alarm clock. There were times, however, when my clock called and I failed to respond. The result was that I remained in bed. The further result was that the next morning it failed to wake me. Felix might have risen into newness of life, if he had only responded to Paul's appeal.

But, though deeply moved, Felix was not willing to pay the price. There was a woman at his side more hardened in the ways of sin even than himself. So far as we know, she was not moved in the least. In fact, I can well imagine that she looked upon both blazing preacher and trembling hearer with superior scorn. Felix dared not defy that scorn. Then there was a yet greater difficulty. For Felix to respond would mean that he must give up Drusilla altogether. That he could not do. At least, not yet. Thus when he might have been free, he remained a slave.

His is an oft-told story. Felix belongs to that vast company that come very near to doing something worth while and yet fall short. They are the almost folk whose stories are unspeakably pathetic. We meet them in every walk of life. Bret Harte tells of such a man. This man went to California during the gold craze of 1849. He staked a claim and began to dig. Day after day he toiled, but in vain. At last he stuck his pick in the earth, turned away in disgust, and sold his claim for a song. But the purchaser had hardly turned the dirt into which the pick had been stuck before he found signs of gold. Soon he was the proud possessor of one of the richest veins in all that famous field. He became a millionaire. Meantime the man who had first worked the claim was making his way back home with pockets as empty as the pockets of a shroud. In the after days he doubtless thought how very near he came to being rich, but he was a pauper just the same. Felix came near to being rich spiritually, but he remained a moral bankrupt.

Some fail, as did Felix, because they never come to the point. They feel the spell of Jesus, but never dare to rise up and follow him. Years ago I walked away from a service with a schoolmate. The tides of the Spirit had run high in that service, and my friend had been greatly moved. "I came very near going forward tonight," he said to me with desperate earnestness. Again, as we came to where our roads parted, he said wistfully, "I came very close to dedicating my life to God tonight." But he failed. By and by a destroying habit laid hold of him, squeezed the fine juices from his life, and flung him away. But I can never forget that he almost became a Christian.

There are others who fail because, though they decide, they do so halfheartedly, or for some reason fail to follow through. These dwell in the suburbs of Christianity, never venturing down into the heart of the city where the lights are bright and where the great traffic of the soul is carried on. They are religious, but their religion is of a kind that satisfies neither God nor man. This is the case because almost to do a thing is not to do it at all. Almost to find life is only to find death. Therefore, I am calling my own heart, as well as yours, to a full dedication to Him who is able to do for us and through us beyond our power to ask or think.

II

A WINSOME INVITATION

"Come unto me."

MATTHEW 11:28

MY BUSINESS WITH YOU IN THESE WORDS IS VERY simple. I am not here as an entertainer, though what I have to say should be vastly interesting. I am not here primarily as a teacher, though my message should be instructive. I am not here to lay upon you any kind of external compulsion. I am here as the bearer of an invitation. The invitation is not mine, but Another's. My sole business is to deliver it as plainly and as winsomely as I can. It is up to you to decide whether this invitation is addressed to you personally or not.

When I was a boy, one of the big hours of the day was when the mail reached our village. Those fortunate enough to be present gathered around the little corner that was boxed off in the racket store to hear the postmaster call the mail. He called each piece just as one might call the roll. When we heard our names, we answered and received our letter, or post card, or catalogue, or sample copy of the *Home Comfort,* as the case might be. Naturally, there was no compulsion about this. The postmaster did not put a gun in our faces and compel us to take the bit of mail that was rightfully ours. We could take it or leave it at our own choice. He had discharged his duty by calling our names and making our mail available.

I

Now my position is akin to that of the postmaster. I am here to call the mail. If you find this invitation addressed to you, it is your privilege to accept it. If you find that it has nothing whatever to do with you, then, of course, you have the right to be indifferent and to let it alone. Listen, then, to the invitation; and see if it calls your name. "Come unto me, all ye that labor and are heavy laden, and I will give you rest. Take my yoke upon you, and learn of me; for I am meek and lowly in heart: and ye shall find rest unto your souls. For my yoke is easy, and my burden is light." This invitation is extended to two groups, to two types of individuals.

1. Jesus is here inviting the laborers. "Come unto me, all ye that labor." The word "labor" implies more than work. Work is a privilege. It is a source of great

joy. Nobody can be happy who is not in some sense a worker. Work is also a wonderful safeguard against temptation. The hours of our greatest peril are always our hours of idleness. Then, work is a great healer of hurt hearts. How many have forgotten in some measure their sore wounds by hard and diligent work! But labor means work that is carried on at the price of weariness and pain. It is work that is so heavy and hard or so futile that it becomes an agony. It is work that has degenerated into toil, the toil of the treadmill, the toil of monotonous struggle that ends in lean achievement or in utter frustration.

One day, for instance, Jesus commanded his disciples to enter into a ship and to go before him to the other side of the lake. They obeyed with all eagerness. For a while their little vessel glided in romantic beauty over the silvery water. But suddenly a tempest swept down upon them. The sea was whipped into a rage. The angry winds pounded them; and row as they might, they could make no progress. The work of the beginning was now changed into toil. They were straining far harder than when the sea was calm, but they were getting nowhere. Strain as they might, all they got out of it was weariness, blistered palms, frustration, and defeat.

Possibly some of you feel yourselves in this class. You have taken life seriously. You have tried hard to be and to do your best. But your efforts seem to have brought you little or nothing. The whole struggle has resulted mainly in vanity and vexation of spirit. A woman came to my study sometime ago, glared at me in desperate fashion, and said, "I feel like I want to hurt somebody. I would like to hurt you." Then, after a pause, she went on, "I have tried to be a Christian. I have worked hard in the church. I have tried to make a Christian out of my son, but he is not a Christian. He is a criminal. That is all my efforts have come to, and I am going to quit. I tell you that right now, I am never going to come to church again. I am never going to pray again." Poor broken and defeated thing! Hers is an extreme case, I know. But perchance some of you can sympathize with her. If life for you has become a task too hard to manage, if you are carrying on with an effort that has in it a bit of agony, the agony of a too bitter struggle or of defeat, then yours is one of the names that Jesus is calling.

2. The second group that is invited is the burdened. "Come unto me, all ye that are weary and heavy laden." If you have come to God's house struggling under a weighty load, then this invitation is meant for you. This is the case regardless of what that load may be. Your burden may not be like that of the man at your side; it may not be like that of the minister; but the chances are that most of us here present are conscious of carrying some kind of burden.

Yours may be a burden of anxiety. You may be tormented by fear. You look to tomorrow and turn hot and cold with fright. Maybe you fear for yourself. Your income is uncertain. Your position is insecure. Your health is failing. Pain is walking with fire-shod feet along every nerve of your body. Or maybe you fear for another who is dearer to you than your own life. Maybe that one is slipping into an untimely grave. Worse still, maybe sin has taken him captive and is robbing him of all moral and spiritual beauty. Yours may be a burden of fear.

Then, you may be struggling under a burden of sorrow and disappointment. You once dreamed great dreams, but they have come to nothing. You have traveled a road that promised to lead to great and worth-while adventure, but it has led to a quagmire or to a desert. Perhaps death has slipped into your family circle and has taken one who was so dear that life has seemed empty since he has gone. Perhaps you have been robbed by an enemy even worse than death. Anyway, you have become acquainted with tears; and you are here, bearing your burden of sorrow.

There are others whose burden is that of self-will. Without any desire to hurt themselves or anybody else, these have been bent on freedom. They have determined to live their own lives. But the experiment has proved vastly disappointing. In the *Arabian Nights* a gentleman, out of sheer kindness, took a feeble old man on his shoulder to give him a lift; but once there, the old man refused to dismount. He was the Old Man of the Sea, and he became a crushing weight upon the shoulders of the one that had sought to befriend him. But self-will is a burden even heavier than the Old Man of the Sea. All toilers, then, and all burden-bearers are included in this invitation. I have an idea that includes about all of us.

II

What does Jesus invite us to do? His invitation is twofold.

1. He says, "Come unto me." This is an invitation that careless handling has left a bit tarnished. Familiarity has, in some cases, bred contempt. It is possible to say, "Come to Jesus," in such a fashion as to repel rather than to woo and to win. But we must not allow its careless handling to rob us of its deep and enriching meaning. There are some ultra-moderns who even laugh at this winsome word; but, in spite of that, it is unspeakably rich to all who will give it a hearing.

This is a word that was on the lips of Jesus again and again. He could never see a crowd without holding his hands out to them, as a mother might hold hers to a tired and frightened child, and saying, "Come to me." He meant something when he said it. He means something still. He means that we can come. We can do so instantly, in the twinkling of an eye. This is an invitation to us to accept his lordship, to enlist in his service, to become his disciples. "Come unto me, all ye that labor and are heavy laden." Every man of us may accept that invitation, here and now, if we will.

2. But not only does he say, "Come unto me," but,

"Take my yoke." This word is capable of two interpretations. It may mean, "Accept the yoke that I give; submit to my authority." But perhaps the better interpretation is this: "Take the yoke that I bear." The one, "Come unto me," calls for a single act of decision; the other, "Take my yoke," for a dedicated life. Jesus himself bore a yoke. He invites you and me, and all the toil-worn and the burdened, to accept the yoke that he himself bears. This first word, then, "Come unto me," is an invitation to enlist. The second, "Take my yoke," is an invitation to share in the campaign.

What was the yoke of Jesus? It was the yoke of complete surrender to the will of God. The life of Jesus was a dedicated life. He lived every day and every hour within the will of God. He emphasizes this fact over and over again. "He that hath sent me is with me: the Father hath not left me alone; because I do always those things that please him." "I came down from heaven, not to do mine own will, but the will of him that sent me." When he was sitting by the well-curb and his disciples were urging him to eat, he replied, "My meat is to do the will of him that sent me, and to finish his work." Then, when he stood at the end of the journey and his earthly life lay behind him, he faced his Father with these words, "I have glorified thee on the earth: I have finished the work which thou gavest me to do." We are invited, then, to come to Jesus and to take upon ourselves the yoke that he bears.

III

Then, our Lord gives us certain reasons for accepting this invitation. He will not undertake to force his yoke upon us. Whether we come and accept his yoke or not is purely optional. He has too great a respect for personality to undertake to force us. He could not if he would. He would not if he could. He will never compel any man to come to him. He will not compel any man to bear his yoke. All he will ever do is invite. Whether we accept or not is up to us.

But though it is our privilege either to accept or to reject the yoke of Jesus, it is not our privilege to reject all yokes. The most that is offered us is a choice of yokes. If we refuse his yoke, then we must in the nature of things bear some yoke. "Choose ye this day whom ye will serve," said a warrior of the long ago. By this he meant that we are going to serve somebody or something. We can choose the service of Christ if we will. But if we refuse his yoke, another yoke, that of self or sin, will be forced upon us. Every man must bear some kind of yoke. It is optional whether we bear the yoke of Jesus or not. But, having refused his yoke, the bearing of another yoke is not optional. Some yoke, I repeat, we must bear whether we wish it or not.

Why, then, are we to bear the yoke of Jesus? The reason given by the Master is a bit surprising. It is not what we should have expected. He does not urge us to bear his yoke because by so doing we may make our way to heaven. That is no doubt the case. The bearing of his yoke will certainly do this for us. But that is not the reason offered by our Lord. No more does he urge his yoke upon us because the bearing of it will lead to our highest usefulness. This is also the case. But that is not the reason that he gives.

Why, then, I repeat, does he urge his yoke upon us? For this strange reason: "My yoke is easy," or "kindly," as Moffatt translates it, "and my burden is light." Jesus is here speaking out of his own experience. Having worn the yoke of a dedicated life, he commends that yoke to us. "I have found the bearing of this yoke easy and kindly," he says. How strange! Why, the bearing of it cost him everything. It made of his life one long self-giving. It caused him to be a Man of Sorrows and acquainted with grief. It meant for him the tragedy of Gethsemane and Calvary and Joseph's grave. It led him to that exceeding bitter cry, "My God, my God, why hast thou forsaken me?" But in spite of all this, he declares that his yoke is easy.

Not only does he make this claim, but his whole life bears out the truth of it. If his life was one long crucifixion, it was still the most radiantly joyful that was ever lived on this planet. In his last prayer with his friends, he makes this request for them, "that the joy that is mine may be theirs." In spite of the fact that he is under the shadow of the cross, he has a present joy that is so boundlessly rich that he longs that those he loves may possess it. Then he has a peace that knows no bounds. That, too, he bequeaths to his friends as he goes away. "Peace I leave with you, my peace I give unto you." Speaking out of his own rich experience, he says to all of us, "My yoke is easy. My yoke is kindly."

IV

Why is this the case?

1. The yoke of Jesus is kindly because the bearing of it brings us rest. The rest here spoken of is not the rest of idleness. That is not in the strictest sense rest at all. While conducting a funeral recently, I noticed that the casket had upon it these words: "At rest." But I must confess that they made no great appeal to me. I have never been quite so weary as to long for that kind of rest. The rest that Jesus offers is not rest from the yoke, but rest under the yoke. It is a rest that is born of right relations, that results naturally from rightness with God, rightness with ourselves, and rightness with our fellows. It is a rest that will keep work from becoming the agony of toil. When perfect, it will enable us to "work for an age at a sitting and never be tired at all."

2. His yoke is easy because it is borne from a great motive. The lightest task may be sheer drudgery if we have no high reason for the doing of it. But the heaviest task becomes sheer poetry if done from a great motive. Jesus found his yoke easy because he cared. He had a burning passion for God, and a burning pas-

sion for men. Therefore, it was a joy to serve them. "For the joy that was set before him," the joy of helping, he "endured the cross, despising the shame." Love always delights to serve. The only time that love's heart breaks is when it can no longer serve.

Some years ago the sweet angel of relief came to an afflicted boy near my home in Tennessee. That boy had been for years a great sufferer and a constant care, especially to his mother. Sometimes she would sit and hold him in her arms all the long night through. Therefore, when death touched him into peace, some said, "Of course, his mother will grieve, but what a relief!" But this is what she said to her minister: "My little boy has gone, and I cannot get to do anything for him any more." She had borne a heavy yoke, but it was easy because it was borne from a great motive.

3. Then, the yoke of Jesus is easy because it fits. More than one team of oxen had been driven before the little shop where Jesus worked to have a new yoke fitted. The Carpenter saw how the old yoke had wounded their necks until the drawing of the lightest load was painful. What was the matter? The yoke did not fit. Jesus saw to it that the yoke he made would never wound, because it was a perfect fit.

Some of us are suffering from sore wounds, wounds of the conscience and wounds of the heart. What is the matter? We have been wearing a yoke that does not fit. There is no surer road to wretchedness than that. A brilliant graduate in one of our leading uni-

versities took his life a few years ago. He left a
letter that was a literary gem. In giving his reason
for his rash deed, he said, "I have grown so utterly
tired of doing as I please that I long to bathe my weary
soul in the ether of eternity." Why had he become so
weary? It was not the weight of his yoke. His weariness rather was born of the fact that his yoke did not
fit. That ill-fitting yoke made him so wretched that he
could not bear to live. Only one yoke fits us; that is
the yoke of Jesus.

4. Finally, his yoke is easy, as another has pointed
it out, because it is one that is shared. In Ian
Maclaren's beautiful story, "His Mother's Sermon,"
the mother makes this appeal to her son: "If Christ
offers you his cross, you will accept it, because he always carries the heavy end himself." That is true.
When he offers us his yoke, he carries the heavy end.
Not only so, but that yoke becomes a bond of union
between him and us. It becomes a medium through
which his amazing power and helpfulness is trans-
mitted to ourselves. Sharing the yoke with him, we
shout with Paul, "I can do all things through Christ
which strengtheneth me."

This, then, is the invitation that I am sent to deliver.
Bear in mind that it is not mine, but his whose I am
and whom I am seeking to serve. Therefore, it is my
earnest hope and prayer that you may be able to look
past the minister into the face of him who gives this
invitation and who pledges himself to make good its

every promise. He is standing in our midst at this moment, holding out his hands to us, and saying what he said to burdened, weary, and flustered souls in the long ago, "Come unto me, all ye that labor and are heavy laden, and I will give you rest. Take my yoke upon you, and learn of me; for I am meek and lowly in heart: and ye shall find rest unto your souls. For my yoke is easy, and my burden is light." This is his winsome appeal to all of us. What response have you made? What response will you make today?

III

A GOOD SPORTSMAN

"If anyone takes part in an athletic contest, he gets no prize unless he obeys the rules." (WEYMOUTH.)

II TIMOTHY 2:5

PAUL HAD A FIGHTING HEART. HIS VOCABULARY IS not that of the cloister. It is that of the barracks and of the athletic field. He thought of himself and of his fellow-Christians as engaged in the most exciting of all games, the most exacting of all conflicts. Now he is a member of the track team. He is running with every muscle astrut to win the prize. "I so run, not as uncertainly." Again he is a boxer. "So fight I, not as one that beateth the air." The game he was playing, the fight he was making, demanded all the high daring and courage required of the soldier and the athlete. And Paul felt that he and his fellow-saints were not the least inferior in this respect. "We Christians are not cowards," he declares with a kind of holy swagger. "In point of sportsmanship, we are no whit behind the best athletes." Let us think, then, of the characteristics that go to make a good sportsman in the Christian sense.

I

The first characteristic of a good sportsman is that he takes part in the game. The team of which Paul was a part was out to change the world. It was seeking no less a goal than the bringing in of the kingdom of God. Paul regarded it as his solemn obligation to have a part in this game. He could do no less and discharge his obligation to God and man. "Woe is me," we hear him saying, "if I preach not, if I fail to play the game." But to have a part in this game was more than a duty. It was a high privilege. He could never think of it without a thrill of sheer joy. "Unto me," he shouts in glad amazement, "is this grace given, that I should preach the unsearchable riches of Christ." To have a part in such a contest was to Paul the highest possible privilege. It ought to be for you and me. No man can come to his best by merely standing on the side line and criticising the players.

But in spite of this fact, there are those who refuse to play. There are those, for instance, who excuse themselves on the grounds that they do not like the game. That was the case with certain ones to whom Jesus spoke. "You are like unto children, sitting in the markets," he said, "and calling unto their fellows, and saying, We have piped unto you, and ye have not danced; we have mourned unto you, and ye have not lamented." Jesus had evidently come across a group of children that, instead of playing, were pouting at each other. "What is the matter?" he asked. "They wanted to play wedding," a surly little chap answered, "but I told them that was too glad. Then they wanted to play funeral, but I told them that was too sad." Therefore, they stood glaring at each other instead of playing the game. That was poor sportsmanship.

There are others who refuse to play from a sense of weakness. They feel that they have so little to give that they give nothing at all. This was the tragic blunder of the man of one talent. He was proud of his gifts and of the part that those gifts would enable him to play until he realized that a friend of his had two talents, and another had five. Having discovered this, he felt himself outclassed. "I would be willing to play," he said, "if I could be superior, or even equal to the best. But, since I cannot, I refuse to go on the field at all." But a good sportsman takes part in the game whether he is captain or water boy.

There is yet another group that we like even less than those who feel themselves inferior. This is made up of those who refuse to play, not because they have too little to give, but because they have too much. These are the smart boys, who say, "Show me a perfect church, and I will join it. Show me a perfect team, and I will play on it." This only means that these superior souls will not play at all, for no team is perfect. Even the New York Yankees lose a game now and then, and every man on the team has struck out more than once. If, therefore, they will not play with the Yankees, of course, they are far too important to play with a bunch of street Arabs on a vacant lot. But what is really wrong with these is not that they are so brave and skillful; they are suffering from bad sportsmanship. A good sportsman plays the game.

II

A good sportsman not only plays the game, but plays it according to the rules.

Now the mere mention of rules arouses antagonism. But a game must have rules or it will not be a game. It is the rules that make the game, just as the banks make the river. To undertake to play a game of baseball with no rules as to how many men should be on a side, or how many strikes should put the batter out, would end in utter confusion. To rebel against rules, therefore, is to destroy the game.

But in spite of this fact, our generation has witnessed a widespread revolt against all rules. "Write your own ten commandments," one free soul suggests. Why not go on with an equally sane suggestion, "Write your own multiplication table." The fact that two times two makes four is getting a bit monotonous anyway. Write your own law of gravitation. The one that Newton discovered is thoroughly stale, to say nothing of what it often does to airships. But we cannot get rid of the fundamental rules of life so easily. As dusty as the Ten Commandments may seem, no individual and no group can play the game of life in scorn of them.

But here is a rule that, though derived from the Bible, is not in it. It is in substance like this: "So act that your conduct is worthy to become a principle of universal law." This means that we are to act in such a fashion that, if all others did the same, we should build a better world instead of a worse. That is reasonable. That is good sportsmanship. But the trouble with many of us is that we demand that we be exceptions. For instance, we are proud of our democracy. We glory in our freedom of assembly and freedom of speech. We can criticise just as we please. But some of us refuse to vote. Suppose everybody followed our example. There would never be another election from now until the end of time. Therefore, the democracy in which we glory would be at an end. We have no right to treat our nation in such a fashion that, if everybody else pursued the same course, it would either hurt or destroy our nation.

As a member of the family, we ought to act in such a fashion that, if every other member followed our example, it would build the best possible home. But some husbands are such poor sportsmen as to demand one rule for themselves and another for their wives. There are, also, wives who practice the same poor sportsmanship. As members of the church, we ought to act in such a way that, if our fellow-churchmen followed our example, they would build the best possible church. But we are such poor sportsmen that we wish to make our own rules. There are some who give to the church in such a fashion that, if others were to follow their example, not another penny would come into the coffers of the church from now to the crack of doom. If everybody attended as thousands of church members attend, there would never be another worship service. Then, how many take an attitude toward the evening service that, if taken by their fellows, would destroy this important service altogether!

The way we are headed in America at this time, it will not be many years before the evening service is a thing of the past. Thousands of churches are already closed at the Sunday evening hour. I am not arguing for this service simply because it has come to us from yesterday, but because, in my opinion, it is sorely needed. What effect, let me ask, is it going to have upon the moral and spiritual forces of our land when Sunday evening is turned over entirely to social engagements, to theater parties, to night clubs, and to various forms of amusement, good and bad? The only possible answer is that these forces will be greatly weakened. Who will bring this about? Not those outside the church, but those within! We have no right, therefore, as members of the team to play in such a fashion as to lessen our chances for victory

Now, since our game has rules, the violation of those rules involves penalties. A law without a penalty is not a law at all. It is merely advice, good or bad. A good sportsman plays according to the rules because he is a good sportsman. He also plays according to the rules because he knows that to fail to do so means a penalty. In what is perhaps the oldest book in the Bible, we read this word: "Every man did that which was right in his own eyes." Every man played the game in his own way without regard to the rules. What was the result? It was not a golden age. It was an age of mud, blood, and tears. The very roadways grew up because men dared not travel them.

But if, as a member of the football team, I wish to be off-side when the ball is snapped, whose business is it? Even if I do get a five-yard penalty, I can take it. But being a part of the team, I am not the only one who is penalized. All my teammates must suffer with me. It is ever the case. Nobody goes right alone. To keep the rules is to help the other fellow. To violate the rules is to penalize both myself and others. That is true in the home, in the church, in the world, everywhere.

A few days ago, I had a distressing letter from a radio listener. "I am a mother," she wrote, "with a house full of children. Two years ago I broke with religion. I thought I might be better off, but I have been miserably at war with myself ever since. To add to my wretchedness, the children fight and scratch and yell from morning till night. I stand it as long as I can; then I lock myself in my room and curse, and curse, and curse. At night, when they are all quiet in bed, I am sorry. But the first thing in the morning, the battle is renewed. Soon, in impotent rage, I am cursing again."

What is the matter with this poor mother? She has refused to play the game according to the rules. She is, therefore, being penalized. This is the case not because the Umpire is angry with her. She is being penalized in the very nature of things. Not only so, but her children are being penalized with her. A child is intensely sensitive to an atmosphere. In a home where the mother carries with her an atmosphere of peace, the child tends naturally to be peaceful. But where the mother is tense with conflict, as in this home, discord among the children is natural and inevitable. Such a spirit is as contagious as smallpox. A good sportsman, then, plays the game according to the rules because he is a good sportsman, also because he knows that to fail to do so is to penalize both himself and others.

III

Not only does a good sportsman play the game and play it according to the rules, but he plays it his best.

Who wishes to play any game with an antagonist who is not interested enough to put his best into the game? Worse still, who of us desires to play with one who has such a poor opinion of our sportsmanship that he gives us the game because he does not think we could stand defeat? Who wants to see a game where each team is trying to give the victory to the other? Such a farce would be merely disgusting. It is such a spectacle that gives us the only example of divine disgust to be found in the New Testament. What was the matter with the church at Laodicea? It had not gone off the field and quit the game altogether. It was still playing, but it was only playing half-heartedly. Therefore, Jesus said, "I would that thou wert cold or hot, so then because thou art lukewarm, and neither cold or hot, I will spue thee out of my mouth." The half-hearted player is merely disgusting.

Not only does the good sportsman play the game his best, but he does so whether he is winning or losing. There are some players that are most enthusiastic at the time they are least needed. There are other choice souls who are most enthusiastic when the need is greatest, and when their cause seems all but lost. We have an example of these two types in an Old Testament story. The Israelites, cowed by their traditional enemies, the Philistines, no longer dare show their faces. They are hiding in the dens and caves of the earth. But just because things are so desperate, Jonathan decides to make a stand. His heroic effort wins results that are a surprise even to himself. Soon he has the foe on the run. What then? These shirkers that have been hiding, when they see the foe actually on the run, come out and follow hard after them for battle. They were poor sportsmen. A good sportsman fights his best whether he is winning or losing.

Not only does a good sportsman play the game his best, but he keeps himself fit to play his best. When an athlete becomes a member of the football squad, he is put under training rules. There are certain foods that he is permitted to eat, whereas others are forbidden. Suppose I am entertaining a member of the football team. For dessert I serve a juicy piece of mince pie. I expect my guest to go for it eagerly, but he refuses it altogether. Why? Does he think it would be a sin to eat a bit of pie? No! Does he think the pie would kill him? No! He has been told that he might play the game better if he leaves off sweets. Therefore, he refuses the pie because he feels it his duty to be in the best form possible. This is perhaps the sanest test of what we may or may not do as Christians. There is no practice that is either right or wrong in itself. Shall I take this course or not? I can find help in my decision by asking this question: Will such a course help me to play the game or will it hinder? If it will help, I ought to take it; if it will hinder, I ought to reject it.

Ralph Connor tells of a great football game between the two leading universities of Canada. The outstanding star on one of these teams was a brilliant player, named Cameron. Cameron was the hope of his university and of his team. But the night before the great game, he broke the training rules and got on a big drunk. His friends sobered him, and he went onto the field, seemingly his old reliable self. But his eye was not quite so quick, his touch not quite so sure. He fumbled at a moment of crisis, and the victory went to his foes. The game came to be known in after years as the game that was lost because Cameron was not fit. A good sportsman plays the game his best, and that he may do this he keeps himself fit to play his best.

IV

Finally, we are to remember that to play the game, to play it according to the rules, and to play it our best, is the sum total of what is required of us. We are certainly not here to lose the game. But no more is it required of us that we always win. Nobody can win all the time. No team is required to make so many home runs or so many touchdowns. You and I are not here to win certain results. We are here to play the game the best we can.

When the Kentucky Colonels were winning one victory after another under the leadership of Bo McMillan, the spectators used to smile to see this team go into a huddle for prayer when they came upon the field. That was something out of the ordinary. "Why do you pray?" a reporter asked one day. "Do you beg God to take the victory from your opponents and give it to you?" "No," was the sane answer, "we do not pray to win, we pray to play. We ask God to help us to play the game in a clean, sportsmanlike fashion." That is our business. When we do that, we can meet with triumph and disaster, as Kipling says, and treat those two imposters just the same.

Not long ago the team of Oklahoma Univeristy returned from a rather disastrous encounter with the Volunteers of Tennessee in the Orange Bowl. It was a good team. It won every game except this one. But in spite of this, when the train neared the University, the boys requested the engineer to let them off a mile from the station so they could slip away to their quarters unseen. When they were denied this and had to go to the station, they lost themselves as quickly as possible in the crowd of three thousand that had come to meet them. Meantime, I am told that their fellow-students were as silent as a funeral vault.

Now it strikes me that this indicates a tragic misunderstanding of good sportsmanship, both on the part of the players and of the spectators. If to be a good sportsman one must win every game, no man can qualify. These boys had played the best they could. When a fellow does that, if he wins, he should accept his victory without swaggering. If he loses, he should accept defeat without shame. This is what Jesus meant by the story of the talents. When the man who had received five talents came into his master's presence, he said proudly, "I have made your five talents into ten." The man who had received two talents came just as

47

proudly, saying, "I have made your two talents into four." To both of them, their lord uttered the same commendation. He did not say, "You have been successful." He said rather, "You have been faithful. You have done your best." That same commendation he would have given to the man of one talent if that one had only dared to do his best. This he would have done, even though the servant had lost his master's money, instead of doubling it.

The fact that our approval depends not upon our skill, nor upon our success, but upon our faithfulness, should give us hope and courage. It puts all of us on an equal footing. The man with five talents has no advantage over the man with the one. In fact, he often does not surpass him in point of service. It was a member of the third team whose forward passing won the victory over Duke in the latest Rose Bowl game. But it is our playing that counts, not either our victory or defeat. Therefore, if we have played our best, when the game is over and we go home, some may greet us as silently as the Oklahoma University team was greeted. But not so our Lord! He will come to meet us, all enthusiasm, and bid us welcome with these words, "Well done! Well done!"

IV

VALUES THAT LAST

"And now abideth faith, hope, love, these three; but the greatest of these is love."

I CORINTHIANS 13:13

I

WE ARE THINKING HERE OF SOME OF THE VALUES that last. "Now abideth," writes Paul. Abidingness is not a characteristic of the treasures after which the majority of our world is struggling. Perhaps most of us are grasping for prizes that are likely to prove disappointing. This is true, in the first place, because many of us will fail to attain. Few of us, indeed, are likely to win all the prizes upon which we set our hearts. Most of us will find some of our best hopes failing to come to fruition, some of our dearest dreams failing to be realized.

Then, even if we win the prizes for which we long, we are apt to find them less winsome and less satisfying than they seemed when viewed from a distance.

49

Some time ago I came down to the church to perform a marriage ceremony. I saw a car parked by the curb. The rear of the car was almost hidden by a large placard that bore this inscription: "Just Married." Below these words was the picture of an ill-tempered woman and a snarling man. These were glaring at each other angrily. Underneath was written this pessimistic word, "When you get what you want, you don't want it." Well, that is sometimes true, with regard to marriage. But it is even more often true of other prizes after which we struggle so eagerly.

"I have spent a lifetime seeking
Things I have spurned when I have found them."

This is the experience of an innumerable company that no man can number.

But, assuming that we win our prizes, and that having won them they satisfy our deepest longings, there is yet this fatal defect. They will not last. They will soon slip through our clinging fingers. There is no single material treasure that we possess that we must not count on losing. However strong we are, one day we will be so weak that the grasshopper will be a burden. However beautiful we are, the thieving years will steal away our beauty. The most brilliant career will soon come to an end. The most thunderous applause will soon die into silence. Assuming that we are perfectly satisfied with life today (though that is a false assumption), we will not be so tomorrow. This is the case because by tomorrow the treasures that are now ours will have slipped from our hands. Things do not satisfy, and, if they did, they do not last.

Yet, even in this changing world there are some values that abide. What have we that we are sure that we can never lose? What do we possess that neither crashing stock markets, nor failing banks; that neither floods, nor droughts; that neither life nor death can wrench out of our hands? There are such values. There are coins that pass legal tender in this world, and in all worlds. One of these is faith, Paul tells us. Another is hope. Another is love. These are values that will last forever. "But the greatest of these," says the Apostle, "is love." Drummond preached a sermon, years ago, on "The Greatest Thing in the World." That sermon has lived to this day. But its title was not original with Drummond, but with Paul. It is about this greatest treasure that I wish to speak to you now.

II

What does Paul mean by love?

He does not mean that bedraggled something that often parades under the name of love upon the pages of modern fiction. He does not mean that sordid and salacious something that poses as love in certain of our popular pictures. Love is not a wild dream of pleasure, nor a madness of desire. No more is it a gushing fondness or a maudlin sentiment. Paul thinks of love as something far finer than all these.

51

Nor is the Apostle thinking of the privilege of being loved, priceless as that is, and as poor as are those who are unloved. One of the most pathetic pictures in fiction, I think, is that of Jean Valjean after he has lost Cosette. Cosette, you remember, had been given to him in her young and tender years. He had been both father and mother to her. From an abused and neglected little girl he had watched her grow into winsome womanhood. Now she has married and gone from him. But that is not so bad; the supreme tragedy is that her husband has poisoned her mind against her foster-father so that he dares not visit her any more. But he loves her too well to give her up. Though he feels himself forgotten, this is his agony that he cannot forget. So he tries to comfort himself by standing at a distance and gazing by the hour upon the house in which his beloved lives. But, little by little, he gives this up. His strength is failing. He cannot go on living, because he feels that he has nothing left for which to live. At last, when death is very near, he takes the first little dress that he gave her and spreads it upon the bed. He then fingers and caresses it as a man might finger and caress the tresses of the woman he has loved and lost. "Oh," he sobs, "she is a sweet smile that came and shone over me and then went away."

What is his tragedy? He feels that he is not loved any more. But there is a darker tragedy even than being unloved—that is to cease to love. If the man whom nobody loves is poor, the man who loves nobody is poorer still. Love is something that, getting into my heart, makes it so to beat as to break the lock off my front door and the latch off my front gate, and sends me out to "rejoice with them that do rejoice, and weep with them that weep." To love is to be possessed of a goodwill that is aggressive, sacrificial, and Christlike. To have such love is to possess the greatest thing in the world.

III

Why is love the greatest?

This is certainly not the case because love exempts its possessor from the slings and arrows of outrageous fortune. It is not the case because love always carpets one's paths with flowers. It is the greatest of all privileges to love, but it is very dangerous. If you dare to love, you are likely to spend some restless days and sleepless nights. If you dare to love, you may at times have your eyes blinded by tears. You may even get your heart broken. Jesus dared this high adventure, and it brought him to the cross.

Some of you know from experience the truth of what I am saying. One of the best-known women in America said in an article a few years ago, "I have resolved never to love again." That is a deeply pathetic word. Why did she make such a resolution? It was born of suffering. She was speaking out of the memory of a broken heart and of a broken home. Of course, she was wrong. But we cannot greatly blame her for seeking to avoid this something that had cost her so much pain. She knew that one could no more trifle with love than with nitroglycerine. To love is very dangerous. Why then, I repeat, is it the greatest thing in the world?

1. It is the greatest because nothing really arrives without it. Paul enforces this truth by the mention of certain worth-while commodities that we should all like to possess.

There is eloquence, for instance. "Though I speak with the tongues of men and of angels, and have not love, I am become as sounding brass." Eloquence is a great gift. Who is not charmed by the wizardry of words? There are words that breathe battle into men. There are also words that heal like balm, and that comfort like the caress of a mother. But this is only true of those words that are motivated by love. Epigrams in themselves are worth little for the healing of a breaking heart. Verbal bouquets have in themselves no power to soothe man's sorest wounds. For this purpose the most blundering word of love is worth far more than the most eloquent, where love is lacking.

Next, the Apostle declares that knowledge does not arrive without love. To understand all knowledge, and all mysteries, and have no love is only to be a human icicle, just as glittering, perhaps, but also just as hard and cold. Not only is loveless knowledge not an asset; it is a positive liability. Perhaps the supreme menace that threatens our world today is just this, that our knowledge has run so far past our goodwill. During the days of the cave man love was at a low ebb, but so was knowledge. If the goodwill of this primitive man was dull, so also were his weapons. But today we have changed all this. Our weapons are unspeakably keen and deadly. Our slightest whisper can be heard around the world, but most of those whispers are threats. We can outfly the eagle, but one result of this is to make possible the poet's prophecy:

> "There rained a ghastly dew
> From the nations' airy navies grappling in the central
>   blue."

We are a bit like small children whose toys are sharp razors, loaded weapons, and high explosives. If our goodwill continues to fail to keep pace with our knowledge, civilization is likely to commit suicide.

Finally, Paul mentions charity. "Though I bestow all my goods to feed the poor, and though I give my body to be burned, and have not love, it profiteth me nothing." Giving at its best is a Godlike something. No man can be genuinely Christian and not be a giver. Yet it is possible to give in an unchristian fashion. Of course, bread will feed the hungry regardless of the motive that prompts its giving. Warm garments will clothe the naked, regardless of the giver. But loveless charity is a very defective something. It often proves deadly both to him that gives and to him that takes.

2. But though nothing arrives without love, the least thing arrives with it. The most paltry something takes

on real value when it is enriched by love. The cheapest field flower blooms into an American Beauty rose when the light of love shines upon it. Why, I wonder, have not the two mites of the widow been forgotten long ago? Why have they not been buried in utter oblivion by the avalanche of gold that for nineteen hundred years has poured into the coffers of the Church? Certainly this is not because of their intrinsic value. They were in themselves worth little. But two mites, plus a good woman's love, make a treasure that is immortal; and that we cannot fail to remember.

3. Finally, love is the greatest thing in the world because it has the most tremendous power to transform.

First, love has an amazing power to transform its possessor. I used to know a flippant young girl who seemed to me of about the moral texture of a good sneeze. She was about as spiritually weighty as a cobweb. But I met her again a few years later, and she seemed to have been utterly remade. She was poised, radiant, and beautiful. What had happened? She was happily married, and she held a baby in her arms. From living solely for herself, she had come to live for others. Even miserly and ill-tempered Scrooge takes on an undreamed of attractiveness once love has come into his life.

Several years ago there was an explosion in the Tennessee state prison at Nashville. Many of the prisoners were wounded, some of them very seriously. A friend of mine told me that he went to the prison hospital to see some of these lonely men. While there, he noticed a little hunch-backed woman, with her hands full of field flowers, enter the ward. She was such a wizened, homely little creature that he looked away from her with a kind of resentment. He felt that no woman had a right to be so ugly. But by and by he looked again. She was moving quietly among the cots, leaving a flower with each prisoner. Now and then she would lay her hand upon some fevered forehead. At other cots, she would pray a brief word of prayer. And he noticed that at her approach the faces of these hard men grew strangely soft, and the eyes of some grew bright with the tenderness of unaccustomed tears. "To me," he said, "she was utterly transformed. I felt as I watched her that Helen of Troy could not have been half so fair." There are many commonplace people in the world, but I dare say that no real lover can ever be completely commonplace. Love transforms its possessor.

Then, love also tends to transform the one on whom it is bestowed. Of course, we do not mean by this that love is unfailingly victorious. Love does fail at times to win the beloved. Sometimes one does not love wisely. "Like ivy too, 'tis often seen to cling around a worthless thing." You loved your son, but he broke your heart nevertheless. You loved your wife, but she trailed your orange blossoms through the mud. You loved your husband, but he wrecked your home. Jesus loved Judas. He continued to love him, even when he saw him turning thief. He constantly refused to dismiss him. He knew that if love failed to win him, ostracism would certainly fail also. But in spite of his love, Judas betrayed him with a kiss.

But while love does not always win the one on whom it is bestowed, it will go further toward it than any other power in the world. This is the case because it has in it the very might of God. The man who fixes his faith on force and selfishness must of necessity make his fight alone. It is flatly impossible for a God whose nature and whose name is love to give his backing to such a life. Not only so, but this God of love must of necessity be constantly at war with such a man. The man who trusts in ill-will, therefore, is pitting his puny strength against the might of the Infinite. But he who goes forth armed with goodwill has the resources of the Almighty behind him. A God of love can back such a life to the last limit. He can make of the lover a channel through which his own redeeming and transforming power can flow to a needy world. To trust in love, therefore, is to trust in the strongest something in the universe. It is to trust in that which has in it the very strength of God.

It is hard, I know, to believe in the might of love in a day like ours. Despots are stalking up and down upon the continents and throwing the whole world into confusion. These are worshipers of the god of force, and force seems so mighty. But if we believe our Lord, if we accept the verdict of history, we must realize that the victories of force are only temporary. Napoleon, one of the most devoted worshipers of force that ever lived, discovered the truth of this. He saw it written broadly upon the pages of history. "Alexander the Great, Julius Caesar, Charlemagne, and myself all founded kingdoms upon force and they have crumbled to dust. Jesus Christ founded his kingdom upon love, and today millions would die for him." Love is, therefore, the greatest thing in the world because nothing is great without it, because the least is great with it, and because it is the mightiest power for the transformation both of the lover and of the beloved.

IV

How then shall we come to possess this treasure?

We must believe in love enough to desire it. "Covet earnestly the best gifts," the Apostle urges. There is nothing that God has that is too good for his children. Here is this supreme treasure, therefore, within reach of every one of us. We all, if we will, may become lovers.

Not only are we to believe in love enough to covet it, but we are to believe in it enough to put into practice the love that we have, whether great or small. If you and I begin today to walk the paths of service that Jesus would walk if he were here in the flesh, we shall meet him sooner or later. This is the case because he is walking those paths, even now.

It is this meeting Jesus and letting him into our lives

that is the supreme recipe for love. To admit him is to admit God, and to admit God is to admit love, for God is love. One day two traveling preachers went to a certain city to conduct a mission. They met stern opposition. So extreme was this opposition that they were dragged to the market-place, stripped, and publicly whipped. Then with bleeding backs, they were thrust into a stenchful prison, and their feet were made fast in stocks. "Did you see how torn and bloody the backs of those poor fellows were?" the jailer's wife might have asked. "No," was the answer. But a few hours later this jailer hears the gospel message. He opens the door of his heart to Jesus Christ. What is the result? "He took them the same hour of the night, and washed their stripes." With the coming of Jesus, love has come, that love that always has a seeing eye and a tender hand. Here, then, is a treasure that lasts. It is as eternal as God. "And now abideth faith, hope, love, these three; but the greatest of these is love."

V

GOD'S ENDLESS QUEST

"The eyes of the Lord run to and fro throughout the whole earth, to show himself strong in the behalf of them whose heart is perfect toward him."

II CHRONICLES 16:9

WHAT A BRACING AND WINSOME WORD THIS IS! The book of Second Chronicles is a rather prosaic book, but here it breaks into exquisite poetry. Here is a gospel as fresh and appealing as that of the New Testament. This word thrills and heartens us because of the light that it flashes upon the face of our Lord. It shows him as the eternal seeker after man. But it heartens us no less because of what it tells us of ourselves. If it lights up for us the face of God, it sheds an equally revealing light upon the face of man. It tells us something that we are prone to forget; and that is that, in spite of all his follies, faults, and sins, man is a grand creature. He has that in him, I know, that makes him akin to the beasts; but he also has that which makes him close akin to God.

61

I

If you are, for the moment, in a spirit of pessimism, if you feel disposed to say something disparaging about man, then you can let yourself go without any great fear of overstating your case. You can agree with the cynic who declared that he could believe in humanity if it were not for folks. You can snarl with Carlyle that the world, as well as England, is made up of so many millions, mainly fools. In fact, there is no ugly word that you cannot say about man, and speak sober truth. There is no trust that he has not betrayed. There is no crime that he has not committed. There is no depth of moral infamy that he has not sounded. At his worst, he seems indeed a very son of the devil.

But if you feel inclined to take an optimistic view, you can do that and be just as correct as the pessimist. For if there is nothing too bad to say about man, it is equally true that there is nothing too good to say about him. There is no danger that he has not dared. There are no heights that he has not undertaken to scale. There is no costly sacrifice that he has not been glad to make. He has crossed all seas, penetrated all forests, left his consecrated ashes upon all shores. If there is much of clay in him, there is also much of fine gold. If he is a son of Adam, he is also a son of God.

One mark of man's greatness is that he is possessed of an insatiable hunger for God. Other creatures are content so long as their physical needs are met. But this is not the case with man. When the Prodigal had spent his all, and was sent into the field to feed the swine, he and the swine had something in common. They both had to eat. But when the swine had eaten their husks, they were satisfied. They could then lie down in perfect content. But for the Prodigal this was impossible. He was haunted by home voices and home memories. "Lord," sang an ancient poet, "Thou hast been our dwelling place." God is the heart's true home, and we are forever homesick so long as we are away from him. This hunger and thirst after God is universal. It belongs to the best of men. It belongs also to the worst. The chief difference between the best and the worst, in this respect, is that the best know that it is God after whom they are hungering, and the worst often do not. Here is a psalmist who is wise enough to know what is lacking in his life. He knows the one way to satisfaction for himself. Therefore, he sings, "As the hart panteth after the water brooks, so panteth my soul after thee, O God."

But there are others who are less wise. They realize that there is something lacking. They know that they have hungers and thirsts that have never been met. But often they try to meet their needs by wilder parties, or by accumulation of more things, or by grasping some poor second-best. I saw a caged eagle the other day. There is always something vastly pathetic about a caged eagle. This great bird sat with his burnished brown wings folded slovenly about him. He did not even seem to care that he had wings. He looked out upon the world with lack-luster eyes. Had I said to him, "What is the matter with you?" perhaps he could not have answered. Maybe he did not know. But I knew. He was missing the role that he was meant to play. He was not made for a cage. He was made for the sky-land and the upper air. He was made "to bathe his plumage in the thunder's home." Even so, we are made for God, and we can never find rest or peace without him. This is a mark of our greatness.

But the supreme mark of our greatness is not our hunger for God, but God's hunger for us. If we cannot get on without him, neither can God get on without us. Man's quest for God has been timeless and universal. But God has always sought man before man sought him. It is the realization of this truth that causes this author to sing, "The eyes of the Lord run to and fro throughout the whole earth, to show himself strong in the behalf of them whose heart is perfect toward him." We seek because we are sought. "We love him, because he first loved us."

It is this love, this endless quest of God after man, I repeat, that constitutes man's supreme claim to greatness. A few years ago, the papers were full of criticism of a certain woman named Wallis Warfield. They told how she had been twice married, and how in both instances she had divorced her husband and had wrecked her home. Many regarded her as a rather cheap and chaffy woman. But there was at least this argument that there was some worth about her in spite of her ugly past. There was a man that saw enough in her to uncrown himself for her, and to give up the greatest empire in the world. If Edward has any worth at all, then his love argues for something of worth in the woman for whom he gave his very all.

Now, if such a love argues for the worth of Wallis Warfield, how much more does the love of God argue for our worth. I am aware that it is not always easy to believe this. A certain psalmist as he looked out upon this amazing universe found it hard to believe in the worth of a creature so seemingly insignificant as man. "When I consider thy heavens, the work of thy fingers, the moon and the stars, which thou hast ordained; what is man, that thou art mindful of him? and the son of man, that thou visitest him?" Then the psalmist answers his own question and does it in a grand way, "Thou hast made him," he contends, "but a little lower than God." He is, therefore, a great creature. He is the one supremely worthful creature in the universe. So precious is he that at his worst and lightest, he outweighs the world. Hence, Jesus said, "What shall it profit a man, if he shall gain the whole world, and lose his own life?" The fact that man cannot get on without God marks him as a great creature. But the fact that God cannot get on without him is his supreme mark of greatness.

II

Now, it is this endless quest of God after man that is the central theme of the Bible. This quest is the central theme of the Bible because it is the biggest fact in human experience. There is nothing more true nor more arresting than God's endless quest for man.

We meet it on the very first page of the Book. I am aware that we can make sorry reading of the first chapters of Genesis if we bring to them a wooden mind. But read aright they are as fresh as the dewdrop on the lip of a rose. When Adam through his rebellion had broken with God, he was restless and afraid. But strange to say, he did not begin at once to seek God. On the contrary, he hid from him. Adam did not cry, "My God, where art thou?" It was rather God who cried, "Adam, where art thou?" It is ever so. Hiding has been characteristic of man through the centuries. It is God who has always to begin the search.

Just as we find God searching for man on the first page of the Bible, so we find him on its last page. Here we see his face a little more clearly. By this time we have a somewhat better understanding of him. But he is on the same loving quest. "And the Spirit and the bride say, Come. And let him that heareth say, Come. And let him that is athirst come: and whosoever will, let him take the water of life freely." Thus, when we get our first glimpse of God upon the pages of his book, he is in pursuit of man. When we get our last glimpse, he is still upon the same endless quest.

He is still holding out his arms, saying, "Come unto me."

Now this quest that is pictured at the beginning and the end runs throughout the entire Book. Here is a prophet speaking on God's behalf: "Ho, everyone that thirsteth, come ye to the waters, and he that hath no money; come ye, buy and eat; yea, come, buy wine and milk without money, and without price. Wherefore do ye spend money for that which is not bread? and your labor for that which satisfieth not?" And again: "Come now, and let us reason together, saith the Lord: though your sins be as scarlet, they shall be as white as snow; though they be red like crimson, they shall be as wool."

Some of you will remember "The Hound of Heaven," by Francis Thompson. He felt himself pursued by a loving God from whom there was no escape. There was a certain psalmist that had a like experience. He ran from God, even as you and I. But he was pursued by a love that would not let him go. "Whither shall I go from thy Spirit? or whither shall I flee from thy presence? If I ascend up into heaven, thou art there: if I make my bed in hell, behold, thou art there. If I take the wings of the morning, and dwell in the uttermost parts of the sea; even there shall thy hand lead me, and thy right hand shall hold me."

This record of the quest of God after man reaches its climax in the ministry of Jesus. He summed up his mission in these words: "The Son of man is come to

67

seek and to save that which was lost." He told the story of a certain shepherd that led his flock home in the gloaming to discover that one sheep was missing. Ninety-nine were safe, but he could not let this one silly and wayward sheep alone. He set out into the wilds and sought for that foolish creature till he found it. He then laid it upon his shoulder and brought it home. So great was his joy over his successful search that he had to give expression to it by inviting his friends and making a feast. "And God is like that," said Jesus. "There is joy in heaven in the presence of the angels over one sinner that repenteth."

It is tremendously significant that in his quest for man there is no price that God is not willing to pay. To be convinced of this it is only necessary for us to turn our eyes once more to the cross. The death of Jesus on Calvary is a historical fact. But the cross means infinitely more than one single historic event. Jesus on the cross is God on the cross. What Jesus suffered is what God is suffering, not for a few black hours, but from eternity to eternity. The cross tells of the continuous heartache of God as he goes on his endless quest for man. Truly,

"None of the ransomed ever knew
    How deep were the water crossed,
Nor how dark was the night that the Lord passed
        through
    Ere he found his sheep that was lost."

III

If God is forever seeking man, how does he seek him?

How may we know that he is out questing for us at this moment? God seeks us in a vast variety of ways. He taxes the infinite resources of his wisdom in order to find us.

1. He seeks us through our daily experiences. When you see the sun rise in the morning, God is saying, "Will you let the Sun of righteousness rise upon you with healing in his beams?" As you take your thirst at the wells and fountains of this world, God says, "Whosoever drinketh of this water shall thrist again: but whosoever drinketh of the water that I shall give him shall never thirst; but the water that I shall give him shall be in him a well of water springing up into everlasting life." As you, who are fathers and mothers, seat yourselves at your well-filled tables, and serve the plates of your children, God says: "If ye then, being evil, know how to give good gifts unto your children, how much more shall your Father which is in heaven give good things to them that ask him?" God is speaking to us through our daily experiences, both of joy and of sorrow.

2. God speaks to us through the beautiful lives of those about us. All of us have been privileged to know at least a few who have about them a charm and winsomeness that can be accounted for only in terms of God. All of us have been privileged to know one here

and there upon whose life the beauty of the Lord rests as the sunshine rests upon the hills. I saw such beauty on the face of my mother. I saw it in the strength of my father. I have seen it in other faces till I have said wistfully, "I wonder if God can do for me what he has done for my friend." God seeks us through the Christ-likeness of those about us.

3. Then, God seeks us through our own individual needs. Sometimes we feel keenly our need of cleansing; we cry as passionately as Lady Macbeth, "Out, damned spot! out, I say." We long desperately for one who can

> "Minister to a mind diseased,
> Pluck from the memory a rooted sorrow,
> Raze out the written troubles of the brain,
> And with some sweet oblivious antidote
> Cleanse the stuff'd bosom of that perilous matter
> Which weighs upon the heart."

God is seeking some of us through our conscious need of forgiveness.

Then, God is seeking others through a sense of frustration and defeat. "My inner resources have all broken down," said a desperate man to me the other day. "I have sworn off drink times without number, yet I know that as soon as I leave you I'm going to get drunk." It is not so bad with you, perhaps; yet you are depressed by a sense of failure. The good you vowed to do you fumbled; the evil from which you turned in horror gripped you. Today you feel like wailing with Paul, "O wretched man that I am! who shall deliver me?" God is calling you and me through our sense of personal need.

4. Finally, God is calling us through the needs of others. We are living through desperate days. It is my conviction that every one of us would like to do something to help. But how powerless we are! We remind ourselves of that embarrassed host of whom Jesus told. "Which of you shall have a friend, and shall go unto him at midnight, and say unto him, Friend, lend me three loaves; for a friend of mine in his journey is come to me, and I have nothing to set before him?" There you have the whole tragic truth —"I have nothing to set before him." This host has a guest that is hungry. But when he goes to his larder, he finds it as empty as the cupboard of Old Mother Hubbard. Such is too often our experience. There is not one of us that is not confronted by calls for help, by opportunities to serve, that in our own strength we simply cannot meet.

When this host found himself in this embarrassing position, he was deeply troubled. It is easy to see the marks of care upon his face. Then, his face lights up and his heart bounds with joy. What is the cause? He has thought of his friend. He is not in such a bad plight after all. Therefore, he hurries away through the night to knock in confidence on the door of that friend. Nor does he knock in vain. By and by, he is home again. But he does not return empty-handed.

Just how many loaves he has we do not know. But of this we may be sure, he has as many as he needs.

I wonder if you and I will be thus wise? We, too, are being asked for bread that we cannot give. We are face to face with doors to which we find no key. If the demands made upon us are too great for our strength, what are we to do? Remember that you, too, have a Friend. Through the needs of others that you long to meet, he is calling. It is the testimony of those who have tried him that he is able to change our painful inadequacy into an amazing adequacy. "He is able to make all grace abound toward you, that ye, always having all sufficiency in all things, may abound to every good work." The man who wrote that is speaking out of his own experience. In fact, he declares with a kind of joyous swagger, "In Christ who strengtheneth me I am able for anything." It is such ability that we need. God is calling to us through our consciousness of that need.

IV

Why does God thus seek for man?

He is not doing so in order to cheat him. He is not trying to compel him to lead a life that is lean and mean. It ought not to be necessary to say this, yet it seems that it is. This is the case because so many of us are still a bit suspicious of God. We are still afraid of him. We are afraid that, if we give ourselves wholly to him, he will ask too much of us, and thus take the blue out of our skies and the lilt of joy out of our songs.

There is a word in the book of Genesis that says, "My Spirit shall not always strive with man." God's Spirit does strive with us, but what is the meaning of this striving? It means that we resist God. It means that God is trying to get us to make one choice when we are determined to make another. It means that God is seeking to induce us to take the upper road when we are bent on taking the lower. It means that God is inviting us to receive the best when we are insisting on the worst or upon a poor second best. If there is strife in your home, it means that the inmates of that home do not agree. If there is strife between you and God, it means that you are working at cross purposes with him. The most tragic fact in the world is this quarrel of man with God.

Why, I repeat, is God seeking us? He is doing so because he is so eager to help. "The thief cometh not, but for to steal, and to kill, and to destroy: I am come that they might have life, and that they might have it more abundantly." This God of infinite love wants to show himself strong on our behalf. He is eager to make us strong to stand upon our feet, victorious over self and sin. He wants to make us strong in the service of others. If he fails to do this, it will be our fault, not his. Whenever he has an opportunity, he does show himself strong in behalf of those whose hearts are perfect toward him.

73

But what does it mean to have a perfect heart? It does not mean one that is sinless. It means one that is consecrated, dedicated. All God is asking of you and me is ourselves. "Behold, I stand at the door, and knock: if any man hear my voice, and open the door, I will come in." This quest of God is endless. He sought you yesterday. Before your mother's lips kissed you, he was there. He has been seeking you through all the changing years. It is a fact of today. He stands even now at your door. Perchance he will be there tomorrow. But he is surely there today. He will not break the door down. But if you open it, he will come in; and his coming will give you an adequacy for the business of living.

A little more than half a century ago a yacht landed one evening at the wharf of Inverness, Scotland. Two young men disembarked and set out upon a walking tour. They got lost. Late that night they knocked at the door of a farmer's cottage; but though they plead that they were both hungry and cold, the farmer kept the door shut in their faces. They went to another cottage a mile or more away. This farmer was more hospitable. Though it was past the midnight hour, he opened his door. To his surprise he found that one of the young men desiring to get into his humble home was a prince who later became beloved George V of England. What must have been the shame and humiliation of this neighbor when he found that all-unwittingly he had shut the door in the face of his king. It is your King that is knocking at your door. It is your King that is seeking for you. "The eyes of the Lord run to and fro throughout the whole earth, to show himself strong in the behalf of them whose heart is perfect toward him." He will show himself strong in our behalf if we are trustful enough to give him a chance.

VI

A DRY AUDIENCE

*"Behold, there were very many in
the open valley; and, lo, they were
very dry."*

EZEKIEL 37:2

THE PROPHET EZEKIEL WAS CALLED UPON TO
minister to a people that had greatly suffered.
Some of them had lost their possessions, some their
loved ones. All had lost their native land. And because their religious faith was so closely tied up with
their patriotism, many had lost their God. Therefore,
when the prophet faced this band of exiles by the river
Chebar, so much of sadness and disillusionment looked
out from their eyes that they reminded him of another
scene that had haunted him by its very ghastliness. On
his long trek from Jerusalem he had passed through a
valley where a battle had been fought not so very long
before. After the battle, the contending armies had
marched away leaving their dead unburied upon the

field. The beasts and the birds and the forces of nature had had their way with these dead, so that the valley was now whitened by their bones. Ezekiel's audience reminded him of this weird scene. So much of tragedy and of spiritual death did he see in their faces, that he felt that he had been sent to be pastor of First Church, Death Valley.

I

Look at the audience to which Ezekiel was sent to preach. He describes it in this fashion: "Behold, there were very many in the open valley; and, lo, they were very dry." That does not sound very hopeful. Yet even here there is one fact that thrills. The prophet makes one assertion regarding his audience that most ministers are eager to make regarding their own. What is that assertion?

Ezekiel's audience was a large audience. "Behold, there were very many." As far as quantity goes, this congregation was one to stir a preacher's heart. Every minister delights in a large audience. Nor is this a mere matter of vanity. As a rule, enthusiasm is generated by numbers. Other things being equal, it is far easier to preach to a houseful than to a handful. Then, to preach at our best we must preach hopefully, and we can only preach hopefully to folks. There is no inspiration in mere pews, however ornate they may be. Generally speaking, therefore, everyone who attends church helps his minister. Not only so, but he helps all his fellow-worshipers, as well, even as he hinders them when he stays away.

Now and then I have heard ministers speak in a disparaging fashion of the "bench-warmer." This, in my opinion, is a great mistake. In fact, I intend to use the first money I get for monument-building to build a monument to the bench-warmer. The only way to have a warm church is to have warm pews. The only way to have warm pews is to have somebody to warm them. This is brought about only by those who attend. The people who are with us in spirit never make much contribution in this direction. An audience of ghosts is the coldest audience that I have ever faced. They neither inspire, nor sing, nor pray; and when it comes to the receiving of the offering, they certainly count for naked nothing.

But though a large audience is, as a rule, to be desired; though such an audience generally brings a thrill of expectation, this one was an exception. In fact, the greatness of its numbers made it only the greater liability. This was the case because of the kind of audience it was. Though great in quantity, in quality it was vastly disappointing. "Behold, there were very many." "Good," we are ready to shout. But wait till you hear the rest. "And, lo, they were very dry." That means that this audience had at least two characteristics that made it an audience to depress rather than to encourage.

First, it was an audience without any sort of unity.

It was like those bones that lay scattered upon the face of the valley. The only thing that these people had in common was death. They were divided individually, divided within themselves. They were divided also from each other. They had been taught to believe that God would take care of them regardless of whether they were obedient or disobedient. Therefore, since they had been defeated and driven into exile, they had largely lost faith in God. Having lost God they were falling apart individually and socially. Ezekiel's audience, therefore, was a disintegrated and a disintegrating audience.

Then this audience that the prophet faced was a dry audience. That word used in this connection is rather startling. This is the case because we have been accustomed to think of dryness as a quality that belongs only to the pulpit. We have heard of dry preachers all our lives. "I would never think of striking a match in the presence of my preacher" one said the other day. "There would certainly be an explosion—he is so awfully dry." Naturally being thus dry, he preaches sermons after his kind. Therefore, when we speak of dryness in its superlative degree, we do not say "as dry as gunpowder," or "as dry as the Sahara Desert"; we rather say "as dry as a sermon."

Now, it may surprise you to hear that I am not going to make a wholesale denial of this charge of dryness. In fact, I plead guilty, both for myself and for some of my brethren. Further, I am going to confess that our dryness is often our own fault. We have none to blame for it but ourselves. But, did you ever consider that there are times when the dryness of the pulpit is, at least in part, the result of the dryness of the pew? There are some audiences that can almost change desert into garden by their sympathetic and prayerful hearing. They can make the wilderness and the solitary place to become glad. But there are other audiences that change garden into desert. They can all but force the minister to cry in sheer desperation, "O wretched man that I am! who shall deliver me?"

Recently a friend of mine was telling me of a certain sermon preached by his pastor. He said the preacher made a terrible flop. Possibly he was speaking solemn truth. Possibly, also, this minister had nobody to blame but himself. He may have failed to make proper preparation both of himself and of his sermon. But there may have been other causes. Last summer I went fishing and caught a trout. No sooner had I landed him than he began to make a decided flop. But I did not blame him. My criticism was hushed when I realized that his ridiculous flop was due to the fact that he was trying to breathe in an atmosphere that was so dry that it was smothering him to death. Sometimes this may be the case with your minister. Certainly this is true: The success of a service depends quite as much upon the audience as upon the minister.

Then it might make us a bit more sympathetic to remember that while the pulpit preaches some dry sermons, the same is also true of the pew. We have no monopoly here. For instance, that was a dry sermon you preached when you put on a bridge party for your friends on Sunday evening, when you expected your church to be conducting a crusade for the bringing in of the kingdom of God. That was quite a dry sermon some of you preached last Sunday when the weather was a bit threatening. Then you stayed home and kept your children safe from any possible dampness. You refused to endanger their health by sending them out in what had even the slightest promise of being foul weather. But Monday morning, when it was not simply threatening, but pouring rain, you went to business and sent every chick and child to school.

But the pew can preach some very beautiful sermons. I have heard some from you recently that were as fresh and green as the springtime. Some weeks ago I went to see a lonely man who was almost ninety years of age. He was without funds and without friends. But a husband and wife who belong to this church had been to see him. Not only so, but they had provided him with a comfortable place in which to spend his sunset hours. Last week these good people buried him; but they did so, not as a pauper, but as a friend. Yes, there are some dry sermons both from the pulpit and the pew. But thank God, not all are so. None need be so. We can be alive, you and I, if we will. And being thus alive, we can help to impart life each to the other. And life is the most thrilling thing in the world, just as death is the most depressing. Here was a dry audience; dry, because it was dead.

II

But though this audience was dry with the very dryness of death, neither God nor his prophet could let it alone. That is tremendously heartening. Never does a situation get so hopeless but that some God-inspired man takes an interest in it and becomes convinced that something ought to be done about it. What was there about Ezekiel that fitted him for this task? In other words, what kind of man can God use for the transformation of a desperate situation? What kind of man can he use for the building of a better church, a better community, a better world? Remember that if God is to do anything toward remaking a broken world, he must do it through us. He has no other way. We must be the kind of men and women that he can use. What kind of man, then, was Ezekiel?

1. He was a man in intimate touch with God. "The hand of the Lord was upon me," he declared. How intensely personal it is. The prophet felt, as he faced his impossible task, that he did not face it simply on his own responsibility. He was there because he was sent. He was there because he felt called of God to do the work he was doing. Therefore he was undergirded and strengthened by a bracing sense of mission. He had the backing of Almighty God. If the task was

difficult, he did not have to face it alone. He went to it in intimate touch with God.

This has been characteristic of all those saints whose ministry has greatly enriched the world. These servants of mankind have differed in a thousand ways. They have differed in methods of work, in temperament, in ability, in education. But they have been alike in this: they were in touch with God. That is the secret of power. How does that light manage to shine? Its radiance cannot be accounted for by anything in itself. The only explanation it can give of its brightness is this: "The hand of the dynamo is upon me." Ezekiel was able to be a light shining in a dark place because he was in touch with God.

2. Not only was Ezekiel in touch with God, but also he was in touch with men. Before he undertook to preach to these suffering and bewildered people, he went and sat down among them. "I sat where they sat," he declares. He put himself in their place. He looked out on life through their eyes; he bled through their wounds; he wept through their tears. He was a man among men. Fellowship with men is just as essential to high usefulness as is fellowship with God. It is impossible to be vitally Christian without taking upon oneself the burdens, the sorrows, the sins of one's fellows. Therefore, when Jesus prayed for his disciples at the close of the day, we are not surprised that he prayed after this fashion: "I pray not that thou shouldest take them out of the world, but that thou

shouldest keep them from the evil." The real servant of mankind must be in touch both with God and with men.

3. Ezekiel was an optimist. I am aware that this is a word that has lost its glamour. During recent years, the optimist has fallen into disrepute. The man today who is always looking on the bright side tends to disgust us, and Pollyanna gives us a positive pain. Some of us have turned so many corners without finding the promised prosperity that the man with the rashness to direct us around another would run the risk of positive violence. We do not even thrill any more to Browning's great shout, "God's in his heaven; all's right with the world." We are shy of the folk who see nothing wrong because they shut their eyes. We feel that we would rather suffer than thus to live in a fool's paradise.

But the optimism of the prophet was not born of blindness. It was not born simply of his looking on the bright side. He looked on both sides, the bright and the dark. He faced all the facts. When God brought him into this valley of death among the bones, he caused him to pass by them round about. He saw the situation as it was. He looked all its ugliness eye to eye. Here was death at its very worst. It was death grown old and gray. It was death abundant and multiplied. But when the question came, "Can these bones live?" what was his answer? What does science have to say? What does diplomacy, what does statesmanship? Their only answer is an emphatic no! As the prophet faced this ghastly death, he was tempted to give the same answer. As he looked upon these bones, no other answer seemed possible. But as he looked at God, there was hope. Therefore, he could not say no. He feels that any big impossibility might become possible if God should take a hand. Therefore, he said, "O Lord God, thou knowest."

4. Finally, Ezekiel was obedient. So firmly did he believe that God was able to bring life out of death that he put himself utterly at his disposal. This is proved by the fact that he was willing at his command to do what seemed a very foolish and futile thing. He dared to preach even to these dry bones. In spite of the seeming hopelessness of the situation he dared to co-operate with God in the faith that, even yet, something amazingly worthful might come to pass. Such co-operation is the duty and privilege of all of us. Not only so, but such co-operation is all that is needed to transform our own situation and make a better world. This is the supreme lesson of this vision.

III

What happened when Ezekiel dared to obey God? When he had courage to preach as he was commanded, what came of it? Were any beneficial changes wrought? Did the winter of death still reign supreme, or was it dethroned by the springtime of life? Did the preaching of the prophet accomplish anything? Did he expect it to do so? How about ourselves? Have we lost our expectation? We have come together for the worship of God; will it make any difference? Are we ourselves—is anybody—to be the better for what we do this day? Something marvelous took place as Ezekiel spoke God's message. Something marvelous takes place still when we give God a chance. What, then, took place in this valley of death?

1. There was a noise. How trite that seems! Yet even a noise among dry bones is a heartening and thrilling miracle. Anything is better than dead silence. To have to face opposition is not bad. To have folk, at least some folk, speak evil of us is in no sense discouraging. "Woe unto you," said the Master, "when all men speak well of you." For a church to be criticised and fought is not in the least tragic. The supreme tragedy that can befall a church is for it to become so listless and insipid that it is no longer worth fighting.

Therefore, I am heartened when I hear a noise. Of course I prefer a favorable noise if I can get it. I enjoy hearing of the triumphs of the Church in this land and in the lands abroad. It is wise and helpful to say something good about your church, if you can. But if you cannot, say something, even if it is critical; anything is better than dead silence. Any attitude toward your church is better than a colorless neutrality that leads you to let it alone. A church can receive criticism good and bad and go from victory to victory. But there is nothing quite so devastating as the thunders of silence. Happy, therefore, is the church—happy the Christian that makes a difference to his community.

Happy is the saint who so preaches by his daily life that it can be said, "Behold, there was a noise."

2. Not only was there a noise, but there was activity, organization. "Bones came together, bone to his bone." Not only so, but there was the semblance of life. "When I beheld, lo, the sinews and the flesh came up upon them, and the skin covered them above." What a marvelous change! Had I been the preacher on that eventful day, I am afraid I should have quit right there, and have sung joyfully, "Praise God from whom all blessings flow." But this clear-eyed preacher saw that there was something lacking. What was it? Listen! "There was no breath in them." That was the tragic lack. They were still without life. They still remind us of that deceased brother at whose funeral the pastor said sadly, "This corpse has been a member of my church for more than twenty years."

3. Since there was no breath in them, the preacher continued his sermon. While he preached, he prayed; and while he prayed, he preached. "Come from the four winds, O breath, and breathe upon these slain, that they may live." Life is the big thing. If one has life, everything, in a measure, is possible. But if there is no life, nothing is possible. And as the preacher persisted, God gave life. These dead lived. Not only so, but they rose from out the dust to stand upon their feet, made anew and erect by the power of God.

4. Not only were these shattered and broken fragments of humanity made alive, not only did they cease

to grovel and come to stand in holy self-respect upon their feet; but they became an army. They were not simply a crowd, a mob; they were an organization. "They stood up upon their feet, an exceeding great army." They were welded into oneness because of their common allegiance to a common King. God has that same power still. Our present world seems as shattered and broken as were these dry bones in this valley of death. But in spite of this, there is still hope. Humanity may yet be welded into a brotherhood. But if this is ever done, it must be done through our co-operation with God. There is nothing impossible when God and man work together. With him we may be equal to our situation, however difficult it may be.

This vision of Ezekiel, therefore, is more than a dream. The valley of death has again and again been changed into a valley of life. Wherever men have given God a chance, shattered and broken humanity has been transformed. Here, then, is how we may help to make a new world. First, we must keep in touch with God. "Apart from me," says Jesus, "ye can do nothing." Second, we must keep in touch with men. God cannot save the world except through personal contacts. Third, we must be optimists. We must believe that, in spite of all appearances to the contrary, God still lives, and that the kingdoms of this world may yet become the kingdoms of our Lord. Fourth, we must so believe this that we will put ourselves fully into God's hands for the accomplishing of this high end.

VII

PLAYING SECOND FIDDLE

"One of the two which heard John speak, and followed him, was Andrew, Simon Peter's brother."

JOHN 1:40

WHO IS THAT MAN THAT, ARM IN ARM WITH A friend, is following Jesus? The answer should have been very easy and very explicit. "Who is that?" One might have replied, "Why, that is Andrew. I thought everybody knew him. He is the man that led Simon Peter to Jesus. He has the honor of having been the first, at least one of the first disciples, that Jesus won. Since then, an innumerable company that no man can number have followed him. These heroic souls have crossed all seas, penetrated all forests; but at the head of them walks Andrew. A great man, therefore, is Andrew."

But such was not the answer. Instead this was the tame reply, "That man? Let me think. Oh, he is Andrew." Then, realizing that his questioner was still a bit in the dark, he added this significant word, "Simon Peter's brother." You see, Andrew hardly had a reputation of his own. What little reputation he had was in his brother Simon's name. Andrew was introduced as Simon Peter's brother so many times, I dare say, that he almost came to accept that description as a part of his name. At first it doubtless annoyed him. Possibly he thought seriously of sending in his resignation and going back to his fishing. He perhaps said, "I had rather be first in a little boat on the sea of Galilee than to play second fiddle among the apostles." But he got used to it. He came to accept it without shame. This was the case, not because he was eager to be the least, but because he was out for the kingdom of God first of all. Thus he was willing to play any part in order to help make that kingdom a triumphant reality.

I

It is evident that Andrew failed to make the first team. This is of interest to us because ours is likely to be a role very similar to his. All of us must play second fiddle part of the time. Most of us must play it all the time. On the athletic field, in the home, in the church, out in the big world, few of us play a leading part. To say this is not to speak in a disparaging way; it is only to tell the sober truth.

Andrew played second fiddle not of deliberate choice. There were some very good reasons for his both expecting and desiring to be among the first of the apostles. He had a right to expect this, in the first place, because of his seniority. He was one of the first to become a disciple. What right had James or Simon to be ahead of him? He became a follower of Jesus before either one of them.

Then, he naturally both expected and desired to be among the first because he was part of a quartet, all the rest of which attained first place. Before becoming followers of Jesus, he had been closely identified with Peter, James, and John. They had perhaps played together as boys. They had attended the synagogue together. When they grew to manhood, they became partners in the fishing business. Together they had worked. Together they had braved dangers. Together they had fought the raging tempests. And now they were engaged in their highest adventure. They were followers of Jesus. How natural that Andrew should have expected to remain a member of this quartet!

But his expectations were doomed to disappointment. The three made promotion, but Andrew seemingly stood still. When death had come to the home of Jairus, Jesus took with him into the death-chamber three men—Peter and James and John. Andrew was left behind. Later, when he went up into a mountain apart to pray, when the inner splendor of his deity shined forth so that he was transfigured, there were with him Peter, James, and John. Again, Andrew was not invited. Then, when in Gethsemane Jesus faced the cross, he had with him Peter, James, and John. Once more Andrew was not invited.

This put Andrew in a place of extreme difficulty. His, I think, was the hardest place in the apostolic college. It was hard for him to see his brother and two friends forge ahead, leaving him behind, because they had been so intimate. We are often less tempted to envy when a stranger wins a coveted prize than when it is won by an old friend. We can read of the promotion of one whose face we have never seen without a pang; but if an old school-fellow or a roommate forges ahead while we are left behind, we are sometimes tempted to grow a bit envious. Andrew had to play second fiddle while his three intimates won first place. This made his position quite difficult.

II

What did Andrew do about it? What are we to do?

1. Andrew did not do as some—grow bitter and rebellious. Take Saul, for instance. One day when Saul was coming home from a battle where he had won the victory, some lovely girls came to meet him. They thrilled him with a song of triumph of which the first stanza ran like this: "Saul has slain his thousands." "Splendid," said Saul to himself. "I am going to have that great hymn written down and preserved forever." Then came the second stanza: "But David has slain his tens of thousands." "The miserable shrimp," said Saul. He then proceeded to go mad with envy. He

therefore uncrowned himself and wrecked his life because he could not take second place graciously.

Among the problems that have been brought to me as a pastor, the majority have had to do with domestic difficulties. So many of these domestic difficulties have grown out of an unwillingness on the part of certain members of the family to play second fiddle! I remember when our second baby was born, our first was delighted. He looked at his younger brother with eyes wide with joy and wonder. He regarded him as a new and thrilling toy. But before many days this first-born began to discover that the newcomer was to make a difference in his own life. He realized that he was not quite the center of the stage as he had once been. He began to get indignant over it. One day he boldly spoke his mind. "I am going to send that little old baby back to God," he declared. There you have it. We do not always propose to send those that get in our way back to God. Sometimes it is in the opposite direction. But we feel that we must get rid of them by sending them somewhere, for we simply must have first place.

The most unpopular member of the family, as a rule, is the mother-in-law. This does not mean that many of these are not greatly loved. But so often is this not the case that the very word has come to take on a bit of an ugly meaning. Its very connotation is sinister. I am told that the oldest joke in all the world is at the expense of the mother-in-law. It runs like this: A primitive woman dashes into her cavern and calls to her cave-man husband, asleep upon his bear-skin bed, "Get up! A saber-toothed tiger is chasing Mother." But the rascal turns over and goes back to sleep, muttering drowsily, "What has a saber-toothed tiger ever done for me?" Here is another that is more modern. The following telegram is sent by a son-in-law to a fellow-sufferer: "Mother-in-law lying at the gate of death. Come help us pull her through." Beyond a doubt the mother-in-law has been the high explosive that has wrecked many a home.

Why is this the case? It is not because she is a bad woman. She is a mother before she becomes a mother-in-law. I think the biggest reason is this—she too often refuses to take second place. A few months ago, I had the pleasure of marrying a son to a very charming girl. My wife and I rejoiced in this marriage in spite of the fact that we knew that it would make a great difference. We knew, for instance, that we, who had been first in the life of our boy since the day he was born, would henceforth occupy a second place. Were we not willing that this should happen, we would likely work great harm both to him and to ourselves.

Too often parents refuse to do this—the mother, especially. I have in mind a home that should be vastly happy. The husband, the wife, the mother-in-law are all excellent people. The husband is conspicuously unselfish, but he is kept in a state of worry because his mother constantly vies with his wife for first place.

Both wife and mother seem to believe that he will give his major attention to the one who is the more needy. Therefore, each tries to beat the other being sick. They make a rather restless and unhappy hospital, therefore, out of what should be a home. The mother is at fault. She should be willing to take second place.

2. Andrew took his second place graciously because he realized that a smaller place does not of necessity mean a smaller man. Greatness of position is no absolute guarantee of greatness of soul; nor is the small position proof-positive of a little soul. "Pygmies will be pigmies still though perched on the Alps." Yes, and heroes will be heroes still, even in a subordinate place. Jesus was saying this when he declared, "Many that are first shall be last; and the last shall be first." How silly, therefore, to regard ourselves as inferior because we are called upon to play on the second team!

If you and I had been building a world, we should perhaps have made all the trees giant redwoods. All of our birds would have been ostriches. All our flowers would have been century plants. But God loves variety. He has a place for the redwoods; but he has a place for the cedar and the poplar, the peach and the pine. He has a place for the sunflower and the century plant, but also for the violet and the cowslip. He has a place for the ostrich and the eagle, also for the humming bird and the canary. The humming bird is just as great in God's eyes as is the ostrich. Neither size nor position is a badge of greatness. I have a friend who is an able judge though he does not weigh one hundred pounds. When he was campaigning against an opponent who was a magnificent giant, his opponent declared emphatically that he was going to eat him up. Judge Shrimp replied complacently, "If you do, you will have more brains in your stomach than you have in your head." He knew that the fact that a man plays second fiddle does not mean he is a second-rate man.

3. Then Andrew realized that his business was not to play some self-chosen part, but to play the part assigned. What is success? It is not to achieve this or that great prize. It is to play the part that God has given in the best fashion possible. A band where everyone played exactly the same instrument in the same way would be far from ideal. God gives to every man his work. He assigns to every man his place in the band. I remember some years ago we had an afternoon Sunday school in our church, made up largely of Chinese. These were very fond of music, at least of what they called music. Every year we would have to do penance by attending their concert. I shall never forget one instrumental quartet. Each member of the quartet played the same instrument—an enormous bass drum. They gave a first-rate imitation of an earthquake, but the music was conspicuous by its absence. But if they did nothing but thunder, they at least had this consolation—every man had first place.

Now it does not embarrass me in the least, though I confess it once did, that I cannot play your instrument in your way. I have become growingly contented to play my own. Years ago, as a very timid young minister, I became pastor of a college church. I would find myself getting up before those wise and learned professors with fear and trembling. By and by I began thus to encourage myself by saying, "You gentlemen out there know a thousand things that I don't now. But I know this particular piece that I am to say better than any or all of you. Therefore, I am going to say it with confidence and in my way." Others can do many things beautifully that you cannot do at all. But you can play your own part better than anybody else in all the world. To do that is the highest possible achievement.

Some time ago a commencement speaker failed to keep his engagement at one of our leading colleges. A friend of mine was called upon to substitute. He began his address with this characteristic word: "I have just returned from the State Fair. While there, I saw a pen full of the most beautiful blooded cows that I have ever seen. But there was one blot on the landscape. In an adjacent pen there was a bunch of scrub cows. The sight was an offense to the eye—so much so that I could not let it pass. 'Why,' I asked the manager, 'do you put these scrub cows in a pen beside these blooded beauties. Is it that they may serve as a foil to show off the aristocrats?' 'No,' was the answer. 'These scrub cows are present to give milk to the blooded cows' calves.' " There you have it. To every man his work!

Andrew realized that in God's great purpose there is neither large nor small. To fill one's place! That is success, however small the place may seem.

> "Thousands at his bidding speed
> And post o'er land and ocean without rest:
> They also serve who only stand and wait."

III

Taking this position, Andrew lived victoriously. There are three scenes in his life, in each of which he played a part consistent with himself. Having been won to Christ by the word of a friend, he became the best personal worker among the apostles. He chose a type of usefulness that is within the reach of all of us; and that is, perhaps, the most rewarding. However useful a minister may be in his pulpit, as a rule his greatest victories are won through his personal contacts. This was certainly the case with Andrew.

1. Having found Jesus for himself, he was eager to share his great discovery with others. The one that he chose as the object of his first quest was his own brother. He became an evangelist to his own home, which is perhaps the most difficult field of all. It is also the most testing. I doubt whether one ought ever to be sent to a foreign field unless that one has shown some proficiency in dealing with those close at hand. We read of Andrew that he first findeth his own brother Simon.

Not only did he find Simon, but he approached him in the most tactful and sane fashion. There are methods of approach that repel rather than win. He did not begin by telling Simon what a rascal he was. He did not tell him to stop his swearing and his swaggering. His was the positive approach. He told Simon of what he himself had found. That is always the most effective method. "I have discovered Someone," he said, "who has made all the difference between life and death in my own heart. Suppose you come and share my discovery with me."

Then it says further that he brought him to Jesus. The word has in it a sense of desperate earnestness. It means that he laid all but violent hands on Simon and compelled him to come. Triflers never get far in winning others to Christ. It takes white-heat earnestness for a task so big and rewarding as this. There was a compelling appeal in the invitation of Andrew that could come only from a man who was thoroughly convinced and who was tremendously in earnest about the high task to which he had set himself. Putting his best into his invitation, he succeeded. His was the joy of victory.

2. In the second scene, Jesus has gone with his disciples for a bit of rest by the lakeside. But the keel of the boat has hardly touched the shore before troublesome crowds begin to gather. All day long Jesus with his friends gives himself to his work of healing and teaching. As the day nears its close, Jesus is con-

cerned about the physical hunger of this multitude. "Where," he asks Philip, "can we get bread?" Philip can throw no light on the subject. "Two hundred dollars would not buy enough bread for these," he replies, "and, of course, we have no money." Then Andrew steps timidly forward. "There is a lad here," he says, "that has five biscuits and two dried fish."

What a flood of light this throws upon the face of Andrew! While Peter and James and John were assisting their Master in dealing with adults, Andrew had found a boy who had a lunch in his pocket. He had got into the lad's confidence. He had done this so successfully that when he suggested to the lad that he turn his lunch over to Jesus, he was willing not only to give his lunch, but himself as well. Andrew did not despise the day of small things. He could understand what Jesus meant when he put the child at the center. "There is a lad here," said wise Andrew. He knew that this boy's presence might mean something. When a lad is present, any big possibility is likely to be present, from the feeding of hungry crowds to the ushering in of a new day.

3. The final scene in which Andrew plays is near the end of the ministry of Jesus. A company of Greeks have come to Jerusalem in quest of the Master. They have this age-old longing within their hearts and upon their lips, "Sir, we would see Jesus." The man to whom they make this request is Philip. They selected him, it is thought, because he had a Greek name. Since

they themselves were Gentiles, mere outsiders, they felt Philip would be most interested and most helpful.

But Philip is not sure of the right course to take. Shall he introduce these outsiders to his Master? No, at least not on his own responsibility! He must have advice. To whom does he turn for advice? Not to bold Simon, not to fiery and dashing James or John! He turns to modest Andrew. Maybe he thought these others too busy. Maybe when he has tried to talk to them in other days, he found them aloof, or so engaged with other matters that they could not find time to listen. He, therefore, turned to Andrew, a man who was at leisure from himself. In so doing, he made a wise choice. Andrew knew exactly what to do. In fine consistency with himself, he at once introduced these Greeks to his Master.

At the close of a service some time ago, a man came forward, expressing a great eagerness to work for the Master. "What is your business?" I asked. "I am a commercial traveler," came the answer. "Splendid," I replied. "You are meeting men every day, hungry-hearted men—men open to an appeal. Try your hand in sharing your thrilling discovery with them." But the enthusiasm went out of his face. "That is not the kind of work I want to do. I want to get up a lecture on the 'Prince of Peace' and deliver it to your congregation." But my best chance as well as his is the winning of men one by one. Whether we are first or second, this is a part that every man can play.

VIII

A PREACHER AND HIS BOOKS

"The cloak that I left at Troas with Carpus, when thou comest bring with thee, and the books, but especially the parchments."

II TIMOTHY 4:13

HERE IS AN OLD MAN IN A PRISON CELL. HIS NAME is Paul. He is writing a letter. As he writes a breeze comes in through the window and fans the thin hair about his temples. A shiver goes through his body, but he writes on. Again the chill wind blows upon him, but stronger this time; so he lays down his pen and fumbles behind him as if in search of something. "Oh, yes," he says to himself with a whimsical smile, "I remember now. I forgot my old cloak and left it at Troas with Carpus. How silly of me!"

Then he resumes his letter. "Dear Timothy," he writes, "I wish when you come you would bring my cloak with you. I left it at the house of Carpus. Come before winter if you can, for it is already getting cold, and I see that I am going to be exceedingly uncomfortable without my cloak. But," he adds, "if you find that you have too much baggage, if you are too heavily loaded to bring the cloak and the books and parchments too, then leave the cloak and bring the books, especially the parchments. I can afford to be uncomfortable. I can afford to have a shivering body and aching bones, if necessary. But I simply cannot get on without my books."

I

Who is this man for whom books are so absolutely necessary?

1. He is a man of the schools. Paul was born and reared at Tarsus, a university center. From Tarsus he went to Jerusalem, where he sat at the feet of Gamaliel. He has had the very best training that the schools of that day could give him, but in spite of his excellent training he still finds that he needs his books. It is very needful to go to college, but it is impossible to store up a reservoir of learning during our college days sufficiently great to last us throughout our entire ministry. "Everybody ought to go to college," says Emerson, "to learn its inadequacy." Possibly we have already learned it. If not, the chances are that our congregations have. The preacher who goes to college, then quits reading, will become a victim of arrested development. He will find himself "letting empty buckets into empty wells and drawing nothing up." It

would be far better to read after obtaining your diploma.

2. Then Paul not only had the best that the schools could give him, but he was further educated by travel and by mixing with men. His feet had marked almost all Roman roads. He had visited almost every great capital of that Roman world. He could say with Ulysses: "Much have I seen and known—cities and men . . . . myself not least, but honored of them all." When he encountered the wits and savants on Mars Hill, he talked the vernacular of the cultured Greek as if he had been bred and born an Athenian. But in spite of the fact that he had the best culture that the best schools could give, that he had the best that could come from travel, yet he simply could not get on without his books.

3. Then he had at this time the further equipment that comes from a large experience in the work of the ministry. He had been a preacher for more than a quarter of a century. During that time he had preached to all sorts and conditions of men. He had prepared many sermons. He had written books that will live as long as literature lives, but he did not feel that he could rest upon his laurels. He must keep reading. He must keep preparing new sermons. After more than twenty-five diligent, earnest, and fruitful years, he still could not get on without his books.

4. Then he was a man of vast intellectual ability and of marked originality. There was not a man of his

day, in my opinion, who had a keener intellect. He was a daring thinker. He made the channels through which the religious thought of the centuries has flowed. Stand him in any sort of a valley, his head would touch the stars intellectually; but in spite of his vast ability, in spite of his marked originality, he felt that he simply could not get on without his books.

Now, there are those who seem half afraid to read for fear their reading will destroy their individuality. Years ago an old preacher spent hours warning me against reading the sermons of another man. He said if I did so I would not be original. I must say that I took his advice with a grain of salt; for I could not get away from the conviction that if it were wrong to read a sermon, it would be equally wrong to hear one. Further, I have my doubts as to whether this well-meaning brother had a proper idea of what it is to be original.

There are those who seem to believe that a man, to be original, must think of something that nobody else ever said before. That is not the case at all. I heard Bishop McConnell say a very wise word to a group of theological graduates. "Young gentlemen," he said, "when you begin your ministry, and somebody comes forward after the sermon and says, 'That was a new thought you gave me today; I never thought of that before,' do not be too puffed up over it. The chances are that the individual will never think of it again." To be original, therefore, is not to say something new and strange and bizarre. It is to take the truths that have lived through the centuries and state them in a new and gripping way. The truth that we utter need not be truth that is new in the sense that nobody ever discovered it before, but rather new in the sense that it has been really discovered by ourselves and hammered out on the anvil of our own personal experience.

Those who are instructed in the kingdom, you remember, are to bring out of their treasures things new and old. They are to be as new as the first flower of springtime, yet as old as the ordered coming of the seasons; as new as the sunlight that looked through the gates of the dawn this morning, yet as old as the sun itself; as new as the first smile that dimples the cheek of the mother's first baby boy, yet as old as the human race; as new as the first thrill of love, yet as old as God. The violet is original; yet it is made out of the same soil, warmed by the same sun, baptized by the same rain that makes the nettle or sour dock. The ocean is original, but it has borrowed from everywhere. It is made up of all the rivers and all the rivulets and all the springs and even of the dewdrops that tremble on the lips of roses. Thus the preacher may gather his material from every source; but so long as he runs that material through his own mill and stamps it with his own thinking and experience, it is truly his, and he is genuinely original. Paul, therefore, though brilliant and gifted and original, could not get on without his books.

5. Then Paul was a man of a deep religious experience. One day while on the road from Jerusalem to Damascus there was a blinding light, and a moment later Paul was dusting the desert sands from off his garments and declaring, "It is a true saying, and worthy of universal acceptance, that Christ Jesus came into the world to save sinners." He had been wonderfully converted. Since his conversion he had had a growing experience of God. He knew the restraint of the Holy Spirit. When he was minded to go where God had not called, the Spirit suffered him not. He knew the constraint of the Spirit. He was a man with a fine sensitiveness to God, a man who lived his life in the most intimate fellowship with Jesus Christ. Yet even this deeply spiritual man felt that he could not get on without his books.

Now I am not hinting, of course, that books are a substitute for vital fellowship with Jesus Christ. If one had either to forego his books or this high fellowship, it would surely be his only wisdom to give up his books. But such is not the case. Not only is it not necessary to surrender either, but each is helped by the other. Though no amount of knowledge of books can possibly be a substitute for a vital religious experience, yet such an experience is surely heightened and deepened by a wise use of books. So Paul believed; and multitudes, through the centuries, have been led by their own experiences to share his conviction.

6. Then Paul is now an old man. He is very near

the end of his journey. The executioner is at his very door. Paul himself is sure of it. In this very letter he writes this word: "I am now ready to be offered, and the time of my departure is at hand. I have fought a good fight, I have finished my course, I have kept the faith." But in spite of the fact that he is near the end of the journey, he believes that it is not too late to seek a newer world. He is determined that he is going to meet his Lord intellectually alert and alive. Therefore, he urges upon his young son in the gospel to bring him his beloved books.

II

Why ought we to read?

1. We ought to read for the sheer joy of it. We ought to read for the delight that it brings us "to lose ourselves in other men's minds." It is said of Sir Walter Scott that he gave to the world a thousand years of intense living. What a pity to miss the thrill of all those intense years! Read a new book now and then, not because of its popularity or because of the instruction that it gives you, but for the sheer joy of reading. It may be a book that few others like. Never mind. You do not eat certain dishes just because your friends like them. You eat them because they appeal to you. So give yourself the pleasure of reading at least some books for no other reason than that you enjoy reading them.

2. We ought to read for information. "Reading,"

says Bacon, "makes a full man." We ought to read to know. In explaining the secret of the spell that Christ casts over men, one keen thinker has said that his was the spell of the man who knew. Jesus spoke with authority. Happy is the preacher that on one subject, at least, is able to do the same. Paul in his letter to Titus writes, "Let no man despise thee"; or, to put it positively, "See to it that your congregation respects you. You cannot always command their love," he seems to say, "you cannot compel them to agree with you, but you can compel their respect," and one step in that direction is to know.

What kind of information serves the preacher? I think it might be safely said that any kind and all kinds. There is nothing that we know that we cannot make pay tribute to our preaching. Of course the information we glean must be digested before it can be of real service. It is not how much we read, but how much we really make our own, that counts. "Reading and much reading is good," says Burke; "but the power of infinitely classifying and using the matter read is better." Therefore, every preacher ought to read certain books for information.

3. We are to read for inspiration. The books of inspiration are more lasting than the books of information. The books that our fathers read to inform them would be of little value to us, but many of the books that they read for inspiration are of abiding value still. It was such books that Milton had in mind when he

wrote, "Books are not absolutely dead things. They are the precious lifeblood of a master spirit, embalmed and treasured up on purpose to a life beyond life." Seek out, then, the books that set your mental machinery in motion and that stir your heart and rouse your soul to dreaming.

Someone called my attention recently to that restless and perplexed Lock in *Alice in Wonderland*. This Lock, you remember, could not be still for a moment. It was running hither and thither with utmost earnestness. It was peering eagerly behind every stone, every stump, every log and tree. It was hunting for something, hunting anxiously, almost feverishly. As Alice looked on, her sympathies and interests were aroused. "What is the matter?" she asked at last. "I am seeking for something to unlock me," was the very sane answer. This Lock felt that it had something of meaning and of worth inside if only a key could be found. And the preacher is often enough in the same plight. He wants unlocking, and very often he finds the needed key in a good and inspiring book.

III

What, then, are we to do with the vast treasure of books that the thinkers of the ages have put at our disposal? It is not enough to own them. We must make them our own by reading them. In order to starve to death physically, all one has to do is to refuse to eat. In order to miss all the spiritual and intellectual food found in books, all we have to do is to refuse to read them. To make these treasures our own we must give ourselves with diligence and perseverance to read them.

What we are to read depends in some measure upon the kind of readers we are. Personally, I am a slow reader. I cannot "rip the bowels out of a book in a single hour," as could the great Dr. Johnson. For this reason it is all the more important that I confine my reading to those books that are most worth while. The preacher should read as widely as possible biography, fiction, poetry, history, and science; but the slower he reads, the more careful he should be to select the great living books in these varied fields.

But while reading widely, the preacher should never forget that he is a specialist. He is expected to speak with peculiar authority in matters of religion. Therefore, he ought to major on this subject; especially he ought, so far as possible, to be an authority on the Bible. Paul was anxious above all else to have his dearly loved parchments. The preacher who neglects his Bible neglects his specialty. I was in the home of a minister some years ago for almost two weeks. During that time I never saw him take the Bible in his hands. I knew him well enough to remind him of this fact and to express my wonder. "Do you not read the Bible?" I asked. "No," he answered frankly. "I never read it except when I am hunting a text." The preacher who so reads the Bible is seeking the spiritual impoverishment of his people in the spiritual impoverishment of himself. It is as I read the Book for myself and find a bracing word that speaks to my own heart that I dare bring this word to others, because of what it has meant to me. The preacher, therefore, should read as widely as possible; but he should specialize on the parchments, on the Bible, which is the supreme Book of mankind.

IX

GIVING VS. GETTING

"It is more blessed to give than to receive."

ACTS 20: 35

PAUL IS REMINDING THE OFFICIAL BOARD OF FIRST
Church, Ephesus, of something that they are prone
to forget. "Bear in mind always," he urges, "that it is
more blessed to give than to receive." Or as Moffatt
translates it, "It is happier to give than to get." All
of us need to be reminded of this, because we, too, are
prone to forget it. The truth of the matter is that this
statement is revolutionary. It cuts squarely across the
grain of our commonly accepted views. That we can
hear it without a gasp of amazement is either because
familiarity has dulled its cutting edge, or because we
do not believe it.

I

These are not the words of St. Paul, but of Jesus.

113

He is drawing a contrast between two opposite philosophies of life—that of giving and of getting. Or, to put it in terms of personality, he is drawing a contrast between two opposite types of character—the giver and the getter. Jesus was constantly dividing folk into two groups. Sometimes it was into those that were ready for life's emergencies, great and small, and those that were not ready; or it was into those that traveled life by the narrow road and those who traveled it by the broad. Again he divided them into those who were alive and those who were dead. Of course, he recognized different degrees of life. Some were far more alive than others, but at the long last men were either alive or dead.

Here he divides men into givers and getters. By this he does not mean that there are certain folk who do nothing but give and there are others who do nothing but get. We all play in both roles. What he does mean is that our predominant passion is either getting or giving. That was true of those who belonged to the inner circle of Jesus' friends. Take Judas, for example. Judas was not a monstrosity. He was as thoroughly human as you and I. He was not a good man, but he was certainly not altogether bad. Near the end of his journey, he asked a question that gives us an insight into his ruling passion. "What will ye give me," he asked the Pharisees, "and I will deliver him unto you?" Judas had some fine qualities, but at heart he was a getter rather than a giver.

In contrast to Judas, we place Simon Peter. Simon was by no means a perfect man. He was always deliciously human, and at times fascinatingly faulty. One day on his way to the temple, he ran into a professional beggar. When this panhandler asked him for money, Simon searched his pockets and found them empty. Then what? He did not merely tell the beggar that he was sorry and go on his way. He rather said this, "Silver and gold have I none; but such as I have I give." These last two words give the key to Simon's character. "I give. I would give money if I had it, but since I do not, I will give something else. This I must do since giving is the ruling passion of my life." It is to help us in making giving our ruling passion that Jesus says, "It is more blessed to give than to get."

II

Just what is Jesus saying by this revolutionary statement? Let us not make it more difficult and more unbelievable than it is. Jesus here makes a twofold declaration.

1. He declares that it is blessed to receive. Certainly none of us will argue with that. We have been receivers all our lives, and we know something of the joy of it. We began to receive in our young and tender years. That which made Christmas the glad occasion of childhood was that it was a time of receiving. We thought not in terms of giving, but of getting; and, having begun with a faith in the joy of getting, we

have never grown away from it. We still are firm in the faith that it is a great privilege to receive.

This conviction leads to quite a few ills. It lies back of the thieving of the pickpocket and the highwayman. It is this desire to get something for nothing that makes gambling one of the major curses of our day. It is this same passion that makes us an easy prey to tricksters, and that sends us to overcrowd the bargain counter. It is this passion that afflicts us with the dishonest politician. To get something for nothing from anybody is a great thrill; but to get something for nothing from the government is, in the minds of many, very heaven.

Then, of course, we all recognize the blessedness of receiving those higher values—encouragement, appreciation, comfort. How much we owe to those who have believed in us when the world has doubted, who have given us back our self-respect when we had all but lost confidence in ourselves! A recent magazine tells a true story of four men, two Gentiles and two Jews, who escaped a concentration camp in Germany to find refuge in the United States. One of them was confined for only a few months. But during this time he had been so cruelly beaten by his captors that it was necessary for him to spend fourteen months in a hospital in France before coming to America. By the time his three friends came, he had been living here for three years. He met his friends at the wharf and took them to share his room in a tenement house. This house was run by a hard-faced Irishman, who was at once mother and father to his brood of thirteen children.

The first night that these four spent under this roof was a sleepless night. They had reached America at last, the land of their dreams; but they seemed to have come too late. Something fine had died within them under the cruel fist of persecution. They had lost confidence in humanity. They had lost all sense of worth or purpose in life. One of their number, Walter by name, was taken ill. One night while his three friends were away, he left a note saying he could not be a burden to them, and slipped away into the night. They tried to find him, but in vain. Then they awakened the Irishman of the hard eyes and told him their story. This Irishman in turn waked up every man and woman in the tenement, seventy in all. These were of varied nationalities, but when he told them what had happened they all went out in search of Walter, while the three friends waited.

What was the result? The writer of the story declares that, as he waited and thought of those seventy people whose names he did not know, and some of whose faces he had never seen, out searching for his lost friend simply because he was a man, he found his face wet with tears; not only so, but his dead confidence and hope came to a resurrection. The friend was found in a dead faint near the water's edge. He was carried gently to a lovely hospital where he died a few days later. But the author declares that he and his friends find an almost irresistible impulse every day to mount a goods-box in Times Square and shout to all and sundry, "Thank you, America!" Yes, it is a fine thing to receive.

Then how splendid it is to receive from our Lord! "I will bless thee," said God to his friend Abraham. That is a great word. We all desire to be blessed. We all have been. The fact that, when we pray, our prayers are so largely petitions instead of prayers of communion and thanksgiving indicates our faith in the blessedness of receiving. But as fine as it is to hear God say, "I will bless thee," there is something even better than that; and here we come to Jesus' second assertion. It is better to hear him say, "Thou shalt be a blessing." This is the case because it is more blessed to give than to receive.

III

Is this true or false? If it is false, the fact that it is written here in the New Testament will not make it true. If it is true, the fact that the vast majority of our world ignore it will not make it false. If it is true, wherein is it true?

1. It is true because it is only by giving that we can justify our right to live. It is only by giving that we can win the right to respect ourselves. Bernard Shaw defined a gentleman as one who puts more into life than he takes out of it. By this he means a gentleman is one that pays his debts. Every man comes into this

world with inescapable obligations resting upon him. The first question we ask about any creature or thing is, what is it for? If it cannot give a reason for itself in terms of service, then we reserve the right to junk it.

There is an old story in mythology that says that when Achilles was born his mother went to consult the oracle at Delphi as to what sort of man he would become. The oracle declared that he would either live a long life of inglorious ease or a short life of valor and victory. The mistaken mother desired for her son an easy time; so she dressed him like a girl and hid him on an island where nobody lived but girls. There he played like a girl, looked like a girl; and everybody thought he was a girl.

By and by the Greeks went to war against Troy. For a long time they fought in vain. Then they consulted the oracle at Delphi as to how they might win. "You can only win," came the answer, "by enlisting Achilles in your cause." But nobody knew where Achilles was. At last Ulysses undertook to find the hero. In his wanderings, he came to this island where nobody lived but girls. He disguised himself as a pedlar, filled his pack with the toys and trinkets in which girls delight, and went to sell his wares. The girls bought eagerly, but one stood aloof and looked on with contempt. At last the pedlar brushed away his toys and ribbons and filmy underthings and produced a gleaming suit of armor and a flashing sword. The girl who had stood aloof sprang forward at once, all eagerness. She fitted on the armor and began to wield the sword, and Ulysses said, "There is the hero. There is Achilles." He could tell him by the fact that he chose weapons instead of toys, that with which he might serve rather than that by which he might be served. We too must make such a choice if we are to justify our right to a place in the sun.

2. It is more blessed to give than to receive because it is only by giving that we can give a worthy meaning to our getting. You remember Mr. Livingstone in one of Thomas Nelson Page's charming stories? Livingstone was a keen and capable young businessman who was bent on getting rich. He fought strenuously on the marts of trade, living according to the laws of the jungle, because he was bent on being worth a million dollars. "Why," a wise friend asked one day, "are you bent on winning a million?" "So I can tell the other fellow to go to the devil," was the amazing answer—that is, "So I can swagger, be independent, not feel myself beholden to any man." To win for such sordid and selfish motives has no worthy meaning.

Here are two shoemakers. One of them is a miser. He toils all day at a sordid task with no finer purpose than to increase a golden hoard over which he gloats at night as Silas Marner used to gloat over his gold after he had lost the woman that he loved. The other works just as hard. He is just as eager to save his money. But he is thinking not of himself. He has a map of the world hung upon his wall, and not only there but within his heart. He is bent upon carrying the message of Christ to the uttermost parts of the earth. He is William Carey. He becomes one of the greatest of missionaries. How far apart are these men! Missionary and miser work at the same task; yet their winnings are as far apart as the spaces between the stars. The winnings of the one are made sordid by selfishness, and the winnings of the other are transfigured by a love that yearns to give.

3. Not only does giving transfigure our getting, but it is the only something that keeps our getting from becoming a positive curse. You remember the story of the magic vest. It was a wonderful garment. All one had to do was to put it on and make a wish to have the wish come true. What a treasure! But there was this disadvantage—every time the wearer made a selfish wish the vest drew up a bit and became a little more binding and uncomfortable. But the wearer of this magic garment refused to be warned. He kept on wishing for things only for himself until by and by he was choked to death, choked by that deadly tragedy—getting without giving.

Why is the Dead Sea dead? It has an inlet but no outlet. It gets, but never gives. That is deadly to a sea; it is even more deadly to a human soul. The man who refuses to give refuses to live. This is not the case in rare instances. It is the case in every age and in every human life. We can no more ignore this truth than we can ignore the law of gravitation. Look into your own heart, into your own home; look abroad in your world. If you do this with open eyes, you will know that every man who is living a self-centered life is not in the truest sense living at all. This is true whether he lives in a hovel or lives in a palace. In seeking to save his life, he loses it. If every man who has experienced this in his own life were to say, "Amen," it would boom like a cannonade and shake like an earthquake.

4. This word of Jesus is true because it is only by giving that we are capable in the finest sense of receiving. This is true in our relationships one with another. Did you ever talk to a cliff that answered in terms of an echo? You could get any reply that you desired from that cliff. If you spoke kindly, you would receive a kind answer. If you spoke harshly, you would receive a harsh answer. And there are echoes from human hearts. Generally speaking, we get what we give. If you say bitterly, "This is a cruel world— nobody ever did me a kindness," that is another way of saying, "I have lived in a needy world and have never done a kindness to any human soul."

Some time ago a woman spoke quite critically of the church of which I was pastor. She had recently attended that church, but she had sat so far away that she did not recognize me when I called. Therefore, she said, "I attended services at that church, but will never do so again." When I asked the reason, she said, "Not a soul spoke to me—not even the pastor!" What is the real meaning of a declaration like that? She might have stated it in these words, "I went to church today. There were hundreds of friendly people as hungry for fellowship as I, but I dodged them all and ducked out and went my selfish and lonely way because I refused to speak to a single one of them." There are exceptions I know; but generally speaking, if we give the world the best we have, the best will come back to us.

As this is the measure of our receiving in our human relationships, so it is in our relations with God. Our Lord is constantly putting himself and all that he has at our disposal. The key-word of the New Testament is "Receive ye." Our Lord is not a merchant that sells, but a Father who gives. There is absolutely nothing of worth that he does not yearn to give us. "He that spared not his own Son, but delivered him up for us all, how shall he not with him also freely give us all things?" As another says, "He literally puts himself in the palm of his own hand and holds himself out to us, saying, 'This is my body that is given for you.'" If there is anything in Christ that you want this morning, he offers it to you.

But while our Lord is constantly offering himself to us, we can only receive him upon certain conditions. These conditions are not arbitrary. They are not certain hard and fast rules laid down by himself. They are conditions that exist in the very nature of things. The measure of the fulness of our receiving is the fulness of our giving. When we give all, we receive all; and we can receive in no other way. Surely, therefore, it is more blessed to give than to receive.

IV

Then this final word! How did Jesus find this out? He did not do so by wide reading. He did not do so by hard thinking. He found it out as we must, if it ever becomes a reality in our lives. He learned through his own experience that it is more blessed to give than to receive. His was the richest life that was ever lived on this planet. How joyful he was! How courageous! How full of peace and poise! How abidingly useful! What is the secret of the fullness of his life? He lived more richly than all of us because he gave more fully. And we, too, shall find life worth while just in proportion to the fulness with which we give ourselves.

This is what Jesus meant by the most fascinating story ever told. It was of a young man who thought that the way to live fully was to get rather than to give. Therefore, he said to his father, "Give me the portion of goods that falleth to me." It was not his purpose to grieve his father nor to hurt himself. It was only his purpose to live as joyfully as possible. But, though he got that for which he asked, the end of his adventure was hunger and loneliness and a place among the swine. It was not the degradation of his position that constituted his tragedy. He would have been as miserable in a palace as he was in a pigsty.

But there is this fine thing about him: Having discovered that he had followed a false trail, he said, "I will arise and go to my father. . . . . And he arose, and came to his father. But when he was yet a great way off, his father saw him, and had compassion, and ran, and fell on his neck, and kissed him. And the son said unto him, Father, I have sinned against heaven, and in thy sight, and am no more worthy to be called thy son. Make me as one of thy hired servants." There you have it. His first request, the one that led him to a pigsty, was, "Give me." His last request was, "Make me." "Let me give myself to thee and make of me what thou wilt." It was then that he received the ring for his hand and the shoes for his feet. It was then that he received heaven's best robe and a peace at the feast of the fulness of life. Thus he learned through his own experience that it is more blessed to give than to receive!

X

COMMANDING RESPECT

"Let no man despise thee."

TITUS 2:15

❦

Paul is writing a letter to the reverend mr. Titus, pastor of First Church, Crete. Titus is a young minister, Paul's own son in the gospel. Now, it so happens that the congregation that this young minister has been called upon to serve is not highly desirable. It is not made up of the spiritually elite. Paul confesses as much himself. He tells Titus frankly that one of their own prophets has rightly described them as liars, evil beasts, idle gluttons. Naturally, a minister in such a trying situation needs all the help possible. Therefore, Paul writes him a letter that is rich in suggestion and instruction. With practical good sense that has been trained by much thought and long experience, he seeks to tell his son in the gospel how to make his ministry as fruitful as possible. "If you are to be in the highest sense useful," he writes, "you must command a certain response from those whom you have been sent to serve."

I

Now what response does Paul tell this young minister to command? He is aware, of course, that there are certain responses that we should all like to have from our fellows that we cannot always command. Look first at some of these:

1. Paul does not tell this young pastor to command everybody's approval. He knows too well that that would be impossible. Such is the case still. It came as a shock to me as a young minister to discover that there were certain queer folk in my congregation who did not approve of everything I did. It was even more shocking to learn that there were those who were not greatly impressed by my preaching. I could hardly believe it at first. Possibly I still think that such are a bit lopsided. But these no longer fill me with grieved amazement. I can now be fairly happy in spite of this disapproval.

Why is this the case? It is not that their disapproval is sweet in itself. It is rather that I have learned to console myself with the consideration that nobody has a universal appeal. However good one may be as a church school teacher, however excellent as an official, however gifted as a preacher, there are those whose bell one does not ring. Now, if I see a man in my congregation who is asleep, I will wake him if I can. If I cannot, I will stop looking at him. If I do not, my interest in him might allow those who are yet awake to go to sleep. Hence, I focus my attention upon the listeners. Even so, I win those who do not approve, if I can. If I cannot, I give my attention to those who do. In any case, I no longer break my heart because I cannot win everybody's approval.

2. No more did Paul tell Titus to win everybody to his way of thinking. He knew that would be impossible. This again was a realization that brought a shock to me as a young minister. I was tremendously sure of the rightness of my position on practically every question. But in spite of this, I found folks that seemed just as honest as myself who differed from me. Some differed from me theologically. Some differed as to what amusements a Christian might enjoy with impunity. Some differed on the best way to handle the liquor traffic. Even today, I find those who differ from me on economic questions, on the best way to bring about world peace, and on various other matters. I win such to my way of thinking, if I can. If I cannot, I can still work with them, try to respect them, and refrain so far as possible from thinking them either criminal or crazy.

3. Nor does Paul tell Titus to win everybody's love. He knows that he cannot do that. Of course, he can go a long way in that direction, even as you and I. All

of us could improve ourselves in this respect if we were only willing to pay the price. For friendliness makes friends, and love teaches love to love. I am sure, therefore, that we ought, in so far as possible, to win everyman's love. To do so would greatly increase our usefulness. But, having gone our limit, we are going to fail in some measure.

This I say because I realize that the friendliest Man that ever lived did not win everybody's friendship. As Jesus went about doing good, some loved him with a passionate devotion, but others hated him with a hatred that hung him on a cross. And it was the conviction of Jesus that those who lived his kind of life would meet his kind of antagonism. "Woe unto you," he said, therefore, "when all men speak well of you." By this, he did not mean that hate was better than love. He did not mean that a thorn was more desirable than a rose. He did mean that if a follower of his stirs up no opposition, he is too negative and too insipid to be useful. This is as genuinely true today as in the long ago. Let any preacher or layman today take a thoroughly Christian attitude toward our economic questions, toward other races, toward other nations; and that man will surely meet with strenuous opposition. To command everybody's love, therefore, is impossible.

But if we cannot command these highly desirable reactions, what can we compel? What does Paul tell Titus to compel? "Let no man despise thee," Paul answers. Or to put it positively, the apostle writes: "My dear Titus: Win men to your way of thinking so far as possible. Win their love and friendship, if you can. But above all else, win and hold their respect! Literally compel them to respect you." This Paul considers a fundamental necessity if Titus is to be in the highest sense useful. It is just as necessary for you and me. However great our gifts, if we fail to win respect, we fail in an effective ministry. However meager our gifts, if we compel those among whom we serve to respect us, then our ministry cannot but be fruitful.

II

Now to tell Titus to compel the respect of his fellows is a big order. How is he to do it? In other words, what are some of the characteristics that simply compel respect? You are perhaps thinking at this moment of some individual in whose presence your soul tends to bow in awed and reverend respect. Why is this the case? What qualities does that man or woman possess that make it impossible for you to withhold your respect.

In answering this question, there are certain accidental and non-essential things that we may dismiss at once. For instance, we cannot win respect from any right thinking soul because of our possessions. Of course, there are those whose hands are full of this world's goods who may be entitled to all respect. But where such is the case, their success in mere getting is not the basis for that respect. "I would have you know that I am worth a million pounds," said an irate Englishman on one occasion. "Yes," came the comtemptuous reply, "but not a penny more!" As a millionaire he was worth just what was in his hand, and no more. In himself he was worth nothing. Therefore, he could not command the respect of his fellows.

No more do we respect a man just because of his position. Of course, high position may rightly predispose us. But we cannot but realize that a high position is not of necessity a mark of high character. Harding was elected President by an impressive majority. Bryan ran for the same office three times and every time was overwhelmingly defeated. But there is no question as to which one of these has a permanent place in the respect of his fellows. What then, I repeat are the qualities that compel respect?

1. Sincerity. I mention this first because it is fundamental. Authorities differ as to the derivation of this word. Some say that the derivation is unknown. Others say that it comes from the two Latin words *sine,* "without," and *cera,* "wax." When a defective and shoddy piece of marble was mined at the quarry long ago, there were those who could treat it with wax in such a fashion as to make it seem perfect. But, by and by when this faulty marble was put into a building, the rains and the sun and the frosts weighed it and found it wanting. Its shoddiness was thus made evi-

dent. Therefore, those who wished to sell marble had to give a guarantee of its genuineness. This was the guarantee: "It is *sine cera,* without wax." That is, it is just what it appears to be!

Now, sincerity is not a showy virtue, but it is fundamental. Without it, there is no foundation upon which to build a great life. It implies frankness, simplicity, honesty. It is a virtue that simply compels our respect. One of the finest compliments ever paid any man, I think, was that paid to Wayne B. Wheeler, one-time president of the Anti-Saloon League. As you know, he was a shrewd and able lawyer. One said of him that he never lost a case before the Supreme Court. When the writer proceeded to give the reason for this, he did not mention Mr. Wheeler's great skill and ability, though he had both. "He never lost a case," declared the writer, "because every judge on the bench knew that he would tell the truth in so far as was humanly possible." How magnificent! He was a sincere man.

Is there any treasure that a professing Christian could possibly possess that would be a substitute for sincerity? What can take its place in the heart of the church school teacher? What can take its place in the heart of the minister? Suppose some fairy were to come to me today and offer me the eloquence of Burke, the dramatic powers of Edwin Booth, the musical voice of George Whitefield, on just one consideration. "All I ask you to give for these treasures," says the fairy, "is your sincerity. You are simply to fail to be genuine.

You are to laugh when you are not amused. You are to bless outwardly, while you curse inwardly. You are to dress your life in sham." What a fool I should be to trade! This is the case because we know that nothing, absolutely nothing, can take the place of sincerity.

On the other hand, if we possess this fine treasure we may be useful, even if we lack almost all else. Men can bear with our crudeness, our ignorance, even with the fact that we have forgotten the score and have fallen behind the procession. But they cannot forgive our lack of sincerity. You remember David Hume's reply to the wits who accused him of turning saint because he was accustomed, when at home, to go to hear a certain old minister preach. "I do not go to hear him because I believe what he says," Hume declared with profound respect, "I hear him because he believes what he says." There you have it. Sincerity is a fundamental virtue that wins our respect in spite of the defects with which it may be connected.

Now, to be sincere as a Christian, one must be in earnest. Bear in mind that Paul's message, as mine, is to a Christian. I can conceive of a man's being an atheist and yet not greatly in earnest. But I cannot conceive of a sincere Christian who is at the same time indifferent and half-hearted. One simply cannot believe the tremendous truths that we claim to believe and remain a trifler. That is the reason that Jesus burned with such hot indignation against the lukewarm

133

church at Laodicea. He knew that their moral flabbiness was a child of hypocrisy. A professing Christian, therefore, who is not in earnest is lacking in sincerity. It is impossible for halfhearted saints to be followers of our wholehearted Christ.

Then, this earnestness that is born of sincerity leads naturally to work. Nobody can be a sincere Christian and be an idler. We cannot respect the deliberate idler in any department of life. Least of all can we respect him as a disciple of Jesus. Suppose Titus had said to himself, "This is a miserable appointment. I have nobody to preach to but a bunch of liars and lazy gluttons. Some of these days, I am going to work manfully. Tomorrow, I am going to resolve never to preach without careful and prayerful preparation. But that is not going to be today, while I am here in Crete. It is going to be when I get into a better appointment." Had Titus taken that position, he would have forfeited the respect of every right-thinking man in his congregation, and would have deserved to do so.

Now, I am aware that there is no one of us who is always a hundred per cent efficient in his church work. There are some stewards who make a failure of their high task. There are church school teachers who bungle the job terribly. How can this help being the case when so many can go through church school from the cradle roll to the grave and come out without the smell of any real Biblical knowledge upon their garments? Some of us preachers fail, with the result that "the hungry sheep look up and are not fed." Now we can have the profoundest respect for those who fail after they have done their best. But to fail without trying, that is contemptible beyond all words. This I say with the sad realization that ninety-five per cent of us do not do our work half as well as we could. Of course, we cannot all be able. But all of us can be earnest enough to put ourselves into our task. To do less than this is to fail to be sincere.

2. A second quality we must have if we are to win and hold the respect of our fellows is self-respect. "If you want me to weep," said a Latin writer, "weep first." He might just as truly have said, "If you want me to respect you, respect yourself." Suppose Titus had failed in this? Suppose he had allowed himself to blush over the fact that he was a Christian. Suppose that he had been doubly ashamed that he was a Christian minister, then what? Suppose, as some do, he had looked upon the big task of building the kingdom of God through the Church as one that was too trifling to enlist his full support, what would he have been worth? The answer is that he would have been worth about naked nothing. This is the case because in thus failing to respect himself, nobody would have respected him.

Why were the ten spies such useless creatures? They had no respect for themselves. "We were in our own eyes," they whined, "as grasshoppers," Naturally, since they had no respect for themselves, their fellows shared their contempt. This, I think, we may lay down as fundamental: Folk do not lose respect for a professing Christian till he loses respect for himself. No community ever loses respect for a church until that church loses respect for itself. Think grandly of oyurself as God's child think grandly of your church as a means of establishing the kingdom of God, and you have taken a most important step toward the winning and the holding of the respect of your fellows.

Permit me to say also that this high and holy self-esteem is not a mere matter of conceit. It is consistent with the most beautiful and winsome humility. Jesus was humble. The one virtue in himself to which he calls our attention is humility. "Learn of me," he says, "for I am meek and lowly of heart." Yet nobody ever thought more grandly of himself than did Jesus. Nobody ever had quite so fine and quite so ennobling self-respect. He spoke of himself as the "Light of the world," as the "Bread of life," as the "Water of life." He was and is that supreme essential without which the soul dies. It is thoroughly Christian, therefore, to respect one's self, to do this so intensely as to compel the respect of others.

3. The final quality I mention, I call for lack of a better name disinterestedness. There is no characteristic that we can possibly possess that will go further toward winning the respect of others than unselfishness, that love that seeketh not its own. I know that we admire after a fashion "the go-getter." We say with a smirk now and then, "He is going to get his while the

getting is good." At times, we throw bouquets at such. At times we give them our hearty applause. But such applause is generally fleeting and superficial. It is not the self-seekers that we give our profound and lasting respect, though too often we give them our votes. A very wise man said recently that he had resolved never to vote again for any man who nominated himself! What a fine resolution! If carried out, it would work a moral transformation both in church and state.

Who then does compel our respect? It is above all others the man who throws himself away, asking nothing in return but the privilege of serving. Such a one always brings our souls to their knees. This is the one bright spot in the red hell of war. As terribly deadly and destroying as was the World War, we can never shut our eyes to the high and fine idealism and unselfishness that caused so many of the choicest young men to lay down their lives for their homelands. Much as we hate such needless sacrifices, their high motives command our admiration. Such eager souls, possessed by a goodwill that is aggressive and self-forgetful, cannot but compel our reverent respect. Sometimes, it is true, they bewilder us. Sometimes we do not understand them. Sometimes we think them silly, and even positively crazy. At times, if such are dear to us, they half anger us while they charm us and break our hearts. We often entreat them most earnestly to employ our cowardly and contemptible good sense.

But if they refuse to listen to us, we bow down to them in our very souls.

"Pass not so near these outcast sons of men
  Where walked your Christ ahead! lest you, too, share
  The rabble's wrath! in time take heed! beware
  The woe—the bitter shame of him again!
  Your flaming zeal speak not so rash—so loud!
  Keep on your prudent way within the crowd!

"What if they mark you of his band, and cry:
  'Behold this one, as well!' ah, you should know
  The jeers, the stones, for all that with him go!
  Have caution, fool! Let others yearn and die;
  These broken ones you love with hot heartbreak
  Can save you not! Be warned by his mistake.
  Remember how he spurned the risk and loss!
  Remember how they nailed him to a cross!" [1]

When the "Titanic" was wounded to her death, there was a man on board who was a part owner of that ill-fated vessel. He refused to obey the law of the sea which says, women and children first. As an owner, he claimed his right to be first. He clamored into one of the lifeboats and arrived in New York City unscathed. He went to his club one day, only to see the crowd melt away at his coming. Humiliated and disgusted, he went to London only to undergo the same dreadful experience. At last, broken and ashamed, he

---

[1] "The Way," by Laura Simmons, in *The Commonweal*, New York. Used by permission.

went to Ireland and builded himself a magnificent palace. Around this, he put a great iron fence. Here, unless he has died recently, he lives to this day. But I am told that the peasants as they pass his gate spit on it in hot contempt. His one crime was his failure to forget himself.

Here is another man. He is a Japanese. When he became a Christian he disinherited himself, cheated himself of a fortune. Then, like a bit of a madman, he went down to live in a pigsty of a house, in one of the worst slums of all Japan. There he stayed for so many years that when he came out he was little better than an utter physical wreck. Yet today when he steps on any continent, the windows rattle from sea to sea. He is a moral and spiritual giant of such proportions that he has brought the world to his feet in a profound and awed respect. He has forgotten himself into the grateful memories of countless thousands.

No wonder, therefore, that Paul thus writes to his son in the gospel: "If you are to be of any real service in the difficult field in which you find yourself, you must command the respect of those you seek to serve. This you can do, not by your possessions, not by your position, not by your cleverness; you can do it only by being sincere, by regarding yourself as God's child with a holy self-esteem, by being possessed of a love that seeketh not its own." These are characteristics that win and hold the respect of every heart in every age. And the wonder of it is that they are within the reach of all our hands. There are many prizes that you and I can never win, but this may surely be ours. Therefore, in the words of the Apostle, I pass on to you his high challenge, "See to it that you command every man's respect."

XI

THE STRATEGY THAT WINS

"Overcome evil with good."

ROMANS 12:21

I

THE TEXT IS A CALL TO CONQUEST. AS SUCH IT strikes a responsive chord in every human heart. The desire to be on the winning side is universal. Not one of us appreciates defeat. However trivial the game, we long to be victorious. If this is true in our ordinary contests, surely it is even more true in the big business of living. Every one of us desires to live triumphantly. We long to tread life's daily way with the gallant step of a conqueror. This ambition, I am convinced, is God-given. We naturally long to win. If we do not, there is something wrong with us.

This God-given passion for victory is fostered and encouraged by the writers of both the Old and New Testaments. On the very first page of the Book, we have this bracing and glamorous word: "Have dominion." It is as if God were saying, "You are the climax of creation. You are to reign over all the forces of your world." This is God's purpose, and this man has done in the realm of the physical to an amazing degree. So completely has he triumphed that today "he can outrun the antelope, outswim the fish, outfly the eagle." In the realm of the physical he is an acknowledged master.

Now, this same high mastery is promised in the realm of the moral and the spiritual. Here, as elsewhere, God has made man for victory. When Jesus had reached the end of his journey, when the shadow of the cross was now upon him, when life seemed to be threatening to crash about him in ruin, he uttered this amazing word: "In the world ye shall have tribulation: but be of good cheer: I have overcome the world." In spite of seeming defeat, he had lived victoriously. As a conqueror he was facing the final tragedy of the cross. Evidently he had found the strategy that wins. Not only so, but the victory that was his he makes available for you and me. So the experiences of the choicest of the saints have demonstrated through the years.

For instance, Paul carried on his work in the face of tremendous opposition. There were varied dangers that he had to face. He went to his reward at last with a body that was full of scars. But though the opposition was powerful and persistent, he seemed to know nothing of defeat. In all these things, he tells us that he is not only a conqueror, but more. Language is simply inadequate to describe the thrilling triumphs that he is constantly experiencing. Yet his experience is not an exception, but the rule. Listen to another of these robust saints: "Unto him that loved us and washed us from our sins . . . . and hath made us kings and priests unto God." These had not only found freedom from slavery, but had been crowned. They were reigning as kings in this present world.

Reigning thus in life, they faced the final foe without fear. Death to them had no terrors. It was not a blind alley that leads nowhere, but a wide open gateway into a fuller and larger life. "Thanks be to God," shouts Paul, "which giveth us the victory through our Lord Jesus Christ." He was conscious of the possession of a quality of life over which death had no power. Thus in spite of all opposition, of all disaster, these saints lived triumphantly. Not only so, but they all declare with one voice that such victorious living is at once the privilege and obligation of you and me.

II

But in sharp contrast to this thrilling teaching of the Bible both by precept and example, in spite of the fact that victory is offered, we must face the disappointing truth that it has not become an actuality in many of our lives. How small our achievements seem in the face of the wealthy promises of our Lord and in the face of his glamorous triumphs? For, in spite of all that Christ has to offer, many of us are whipped of life. "For us, at least," we say desperately, "it has not worked out."

This is the case not simply with the moral triflers. There are some who seem not even to try to win, though I believe there are fewer of these than we commonly realize. Most people, I dare say, try harder than we think. We see their failures, but we do not see the pathetic struggles through which they passed before they failed. But though we have tried desperately hard, we are saying with another, "The good I vowed to do I fumbled; the evil from which I swore off with desperate determination I committed." We remind ourselves of a fly caught in a spider's web. Struggle how we may, we fail to find freedom.

As we fail to triumph as individuals, so also do we fail as a Church. Now do not misunderstand me. I speak as a son of the Church. The Church is my spiritual mother. I can sing with some of the fervor of Wesley:

"I love Thy Church, O God!
    Her walls before Thee stand,
Dear as the apple of Thine eye,
    And graven on Thy hand.

"For her my tears shall fall,
    For her my prayers ascend,
To her my cares and toils be given,
    Till toils and cares shall end."

I believe in the Church. It is still my conviction that Jesus spoke sober truth when he said, "I will build my church; and the gates of hell shall not prevail against it." I believe that it is the best institution in the world, and that it is the supreme hope for bringing in the kingdom of God. But I cannot shut my eyes to her partial failure. When we sing, "Like a mighty army moves the Church of God," a note of unreality tends to creep into our hearts. Our church is to be a glorious church "without spot or blemish or any such thing." It is to salt the earth, to save civilization from moral rottenness. We are doing much toward this, but we are not doing enough.

Because of our partial failure as individuals and as a church, there is widespread spiritual and moral failure in our world. Whole nations have flung away from God and are now on a trek toward paganism. Because of this lack of vital religion, civilization is on the verge of the abyss. It is not easy today to believe in the triumph of righteousness. The moral and spiritual forces seem to be threatened with defeat. We may sing with Lowell with conviction, "Right forever on the scaffold, wrong forever on the throne." But too few are so sure that "behind the dim unknown standeth God within the shadow, keeping watch above his own." In spite, therefore, of the possibility of victory, there is widespread defeat.

III

Why is this the case? We believe that much of our failure is born of a wrong technique. For instance, when we set out to conquer evil, we have an almost irresistible tendency to focus our attention upon the evil that is to be destroyed rather than upon the good that is to take its place. In other words, we do exactly what our Lord warned us not to do. When we find weeds growing among the wheat, we squander all our energies upon the pulling of the weeds rather than upon the cultivation of the wheat. Such a course always ends in complete or partial failure. This is true for at least two reasons.

1. Merely to seek to repress evil fails because all nature abhors a vacuum. Emptiness invites an occupant. That is what Jesus meant by that short and striking parable of the empty house. "When the unclean spirit is gone out of a man, he walketh through dry places, seeking rest, and findeth none. Then he saith, I will return into my house from whence I came out; and when he is come, he findeth it empty, swept, and garnished. Then goeth he, and taketh with himself seven other spirits more wicked than himself, and they enter in and dwell there: and the last state of that man is worse than the first." That is, if you drive evil out of the front door, it returns, oftentimes re-enforced, to steal in at the back door.

This summer I went fishing. I had a leaky boat. It was so leaky that, by hard work bailing out the water, we could hold our own. But the boat was never empty because the water kept coming in. This is what happens when we set out merely to destroy evil in our own lives or in our world. However hard we work, we find that the weeds we pull keep growing again. For many years, for instance, the churches of America cultivated an antagonism to liquor in all its forms. So successfully did they do this that at last liquor was outlawed. Then, having won the victory, we left off our fighting. We failed to put in its place a vigorous conviction of the importance of sobriety. We know the result. The liquor traffic is back today, fortified and strengthened. In fact, it has been baptized, especially by our movie folk, with a respectability never known before.

We often make the same mistake in our dealing with crime. We put the emphasis on the imprisonment or the killing of the criminal rather than the making him into a good citizen. The worst crime-breeding spot in our city is known as Southtown. Here we spend two dollars and seventy cents per capita for police. But we only spend nine cents per capita for education. That is, we believe thirty times as much in the efficacy of force to stamp out evil as we do in the power of good to prevent it. Much of our effort, therefore, to overcome evil is futile because it is purely negative. We cannot win in this fashion.

2. Such efforts end in failure because, even though we were successful, our success would bring us to no worthy goal. The most worth-while garden is not the

one that has the fewest nettles or weeds, but the one that has the most abundant fruits and flowers. A distinguished physician told me sometime ago that he was curing cancer, but that in the process he was killing the patient. So what? We do not need a great scientist to accomplish this. Any of us could do as much with a good Winchester. Down in the morgue the other day, a visitor was seized by a fit of coughing. "That is a bad cough you have," said the manager. "Yes," came the answer, "but any of these chaps lying here on slabs would be glad to have it." Certainly! I would rather be alive with a cough than dead without one.

But in spite of this, we still have a feeling that, to be holy, one only needs to be harmless. The other day I was talking to a gentleman about becoming a Christian. What was his answer? "I am not so bad." Then he began to enumerate a list of evils of which he was not guilty. But what of that? The same assertion might have been made of a wax figure or a corpse. We can no more add up a list of "don'ts" and get a worth-while character than we can add up a list of ciphers and get a unit. Our moral and spiritual ciphers may reach from here to Mars; but, when we add them all up, we only have one miserable cipher. Merely to repress evil, therefore, is futile because it is at once impossible and useless.

IV

What then is the strategy that wins? Paul states it

here in language strikingly simple: "If you desire to overcome evil," he says, "do not fix your attention upon the evil, but upon the good that you are to put in its place." Certainly! There is no way to conquer evil except by the might of the good. That was the strategy that Jesus always employed. It is at once scriptural and sane. Of all the commands of the New Testament, there is none more saturated with commonsense than this: "Overcome evil with good." This is the secret of victory in every department of life.

1. It is so in the realm of the physical. Suppose you are afflicted with some disease, what is the remedy? I remember a rather ludicrous passage from Mrs. Eddy to the effect that in treating the sick, she sometimes found it helpful to etherize the patient; that is, to make him to float off into thin air. This done, the pain was left standing out like a mountain. Of course, after that it was a very simple process to kill the pain. Thus the patient was healed as if by magic. But as a matter of fact, this does not work. Christian Science does effect some real cures. This it does by causing the patient to fix his attention upon health rather than upon disease. The only real remedy for sickness is health, just as the only real cure for darkness is light.

2. This is also the only road to moral and spiritual health. We can drive out our vices only by the bringing in of vigorous virtues. The same is true in our relationships with our fellows. If things are going badly between husband and wife, what is the remedy?

Divorce is the common answer. Thus we spend much time trying to improve our divorce laws. But what needs to be improved is not divorce, but marriage. The only way to improve a discordant marriage is to displace misunderstanding by understanding, unkindness by kindness, hate by love. This is the most effective way to destroy an enemy of any kind, whether that enemy be in the heart or in the home or out of it.

One day a man by the name of Burbank met the cactus. The cactus, you know is one of the most disagreeable plants in the vegetable kingdom. It believes in preparedness. It is armed to the teeth. But this believer in plants did not undertake to exterminate the cactus. He changed it into the spineless cactus. Today when we meet it, we no longer gather our garments about us lest it should touch us; but we should like to wear its colorful beauty over our hearts, or rub our cheeks against the soft velvet of its petals. He found a foe and made it into a friend. Jesus believed that through the technique of kindness we could change many of our foes into friends. But too many prefer the negative way of giving hate for hate, or breaking off relations altogether. It is only by the bringing in of the good that we can win, in our hearts or in our homes.

This is also the way of conquest for the Church. Ours is a day when the Church is often on the defensive. Such a course cannot but end in failure. We cannot hope to make a touchdown if the other side keeps possession of the ball. Neither as individuals nor as groups can we hold our own. We live our lives on an incline and must go up or down. Yet I read the report of a church sometime ago that ended, "Pray for us, brethren, that we may hold our own." That is at once a futile and impossible prayer. When we cease to be aggressive, we at once begin to retreat.

Notice how constantly the saints of the early Church refused to be put on the defensive. "Paul, thou art permitted to speak for thyself." Agrippa is giving this great apostle a chance to defend himself. At once Paul begins as if that were his sole purpose. "I think myself happy, king Agrippa, because I shall answer for myself this day before thee touching all the things whereof I am accused of the Jews; especially because I know thee to be expert in all customs and questions which are among the Jews: wherefore I beseech thee to hear me patiently." But how does it end? "King Agrippa, believest thou the prophets? I know that thou believeth." Then Agrippa said, "Almost thou persuadest me to be a Christian." Who is on the defensive now? Not Paul, but King Agrippa! The Church can never win except as it changes defense into attack.

Not only so, but this attack must not be one simply of denunciation. It must be the making regnant of a positive good. It is striking how little time the preachers of the New Testament spent in the denunciation of the evils of their day. Injustice, slavery, infanticide, and countless other evils were abroad; but they gave little attention to them. There was the terrific evil of polytheism. Had we lived then, we should doubtless have given a whole series of sermons to the denunciation of false gods. One Sunday we should have discussed Jupiter, another Mars, another Venus. But these preachers had little to say of these false gods. They preached a victorious Christ. As they preached, these gods vanished, as the stars vanished this morning at the coming of the sunrise.

Here then is a strategy that wins. Remember that there is nothing so tantalizing nor so futile as to try to be good without being good for something. One day Paul wrote a letter to some vigorous and hot-blooded folk in Galatia. These were undertaking the high task of being Christians, and were not finding it easy. Notice the advice he gives. He does not tell them to clinch their fists and square their jaws and strengthen their weak wills. He does not tell them to pull up their vices by the roots, one by one. He rather says this sane word: "This I say then, Walk in the Spirit and ye shall not fulfill the lust of the flesh." Fill your life with God and with Godlike tasks, and there will be no room for the evils that threaten your undoing. When one asked Ney, the bravest of Napoleon's marshals, the secret of his courage, he answered, "I am too busy fighting to be afraid." Even so. All else ends in failure.

The only way to avoid that tragedy is to use the high strategy of the apostle, "Overcome evil with good."

XII

DELIGHTFUL BEGGARS

"Begging me of their own accord, most urgently, for the favor . . . ."

II CORINTHIANS 8:4 (MOFFATT)

EVEN A CASUAL READING OF THE PASSAGE OF WHICH our text is a part would indicate that Paul is enjoying a genuine thrill. He is as enthusiastic as a football fan whose team has just scored a touchdown. He is ready to lay almost violent hands on any chance passer-by to tell him of the amazing and heartening experience through which he has just passed. He is sure that he has a story to tell that is infinitely too good to keep. "While in Macedonia," he declares joyfully, "I was literally besieged by beggars. They thronged about me with a compelling urgency. They pressed their request upon me with a determination that refused to be denied. It was indeed a most joyful experience."

Now, that sounds a bit queer, does it not? As a rule, we do not like beggars. We generally seek to dodge the folk who are perpetually asking for favors. We avoid, so far as possible, those who are forever saying, "Where do I come in?" and "What do I get out of it?" The individual whose watchword is "gimme" is about as popular as a painful disease. While I was pastor in Washington, the Government sent me to the Panama Canal Zone to speak to the operatives. On my way, I spent a day in Port au Prince, Haiti. In a brief walk about the city, we were accompanied by a growing crowd of beggars. It was not an altogether delightful experience. Even patient mothers sometimes grow weary of children who are constantly plucking at their skirts and asking for something. But these beggars thrilled Paul beyond all words! I wonder why?

I

Paul found these beggars delightful because of the nature of their request. They were asking for a favor; this they confessed without shame, but the favor that they were seeking is certainly refreshingly unique. Paul found it as thrilling as martial music; it was as fragrant as the perfume of violets; it was as bracing as a breeze from sun-kissed mountains. He could hardly think of their request without a shout of sheer joy. What favor then were they asking?

It was not of the type that is most generally sought.

For instance, they were not asking for money. Of course, there are times when that is a perfectly right and legitimate request. There are very few of us who have not had to ask such a favor at some time in our lives.

No more were they asking for exemption. That kind of favor is also often right and natural. These people had suffered; they had passed, Paul tells us, through "a great trial of affliction." They had been reduced to the lowest depths of poverty. Therefore, it would have been quite natural and fitting had they come forward and said to the great Apostle, "We are not asking for help, we have refused and will continue to refuse to be a burden to the church; but, while we make no requests for help, we do ask that you make no claims on us. We are going to look out for ourselves as best we can, but that is the extent of our ability; we cannot help others."

Now, there are those in every church that belong to this class. Oftentimes, these are among the most saintly. Sometimes such feel that they have little right to the privileges offered by the church. I have even had these to suggest that they were embarrassed by occupying a pew for which they could make no financial return. They even felt that they ought to remain away. But, of course, such an attitude is altogether wrong. There are other contributions that you can make, if you belong to this class, that are far more priceless than money. You can give your sympathy, the inspiration of your presence, the undergirding of your prayers. Therefore, let me beg of you that you do not allow the fact that you cannot contribute money to prevent you from making any contribution at all. But these people were not asking for that kind of exemption!

Neither were they asking for a position. They were not seeking a job. This, of course, is a perfectly legitimate and right request. Everybody has a right to work. There is no surer indication that an economic and social order has gone wrong than the fact that millions that are willing to work have nothing to do. The denial of the right to work robs a man of his daily bread. But it does something even worse than that. It tends to rob him of his self-respect, to break his morale. Therefore, although these people were not asking for work, such a request is always in order.

For what, then, were they asking? Listen! "Begging me of their own accord, most urgently, for the favor of contributing to the support of the saints." There you have it! No wonder Paul was so enthusiastic. No wonder he could not think of the experience in the after days without a burst of song. These people had come to a new attitude toward their wealth; giving had ceased to be a chore that they performed reluctantly and with wry faces. It had become a joy—it had been changed for them from prose to exquisite poetry, from sobs to songs. "They begged me of their own accord most urgently for the favor of contributing." You can hear the lilt of joy in Paul's voice and catch the sparkle in his eye across the far spaces of the centuries. It is something to thrill over.

II

Now how, I wonder, had this change of attitude toward giving come about? We are safe in saying that it was not theirs by nature. All the people of that day did not regard giving in this fashion. Had they done so, the kingdom of God would have come long ago. All of us do not feel that way today. If so, the kingdom of God would be at our very doors. Of course, I do not mean by this that human nature is altogether bad. Were that the case, it would be altogether useless for me to preach to you. But neither is it all good. We are strange mixtures of the heights and depths, of stardust and mud. Left to ourselves, we do not look upon giving as a privilege.

Neither did these people look upon an opportunity to give as a favor to themselves because they were so prosperous. In the first place, they were anything but prosperous. They were desperately poor. Then prosperity does not always make for liberality. In fact, it often makes for the opposite. A man who is making money rapidly has a great tendency to be less liberal than he would be otherwise. Every dollar he gives, he measures not simply by its own worth, but by the other dollar he could make through it if he should invest it. John Jacob Astor, for instance, is credited with saying a sordid and mean thing. When asked for a donation for a worthy cause, he took a coin from his pocket, looked at it, and said, "I might spare this coin, but I could not spare the interest." There you have it.

The Rich Fool was prosperous. The sunshine and rain had come in just the right proportions; his employees had been energetic and trustworthy. His crops were so abundant that he must needs pulls down his old barns and build greater. He thought within himself, the story says, saying, "What shall I do?" and having considered, he set about planning, not how he could use his wealth for the best interests of others, but how he could conserve every penny of it for himself. Thus his prosperity did not add to his liberality, but rather increased his stinginess.

Why, then, this changed attitude toward giving? Paul cannot explain it except in terms of God. He begins his story by saying, "I want you to know the grace that God has bestowed upon the churches of Macedonia." And what greater grace could even God bestow than the grace of enabling us so to share his nature that we also share his passion for giving. "God so loved the world that he gave . . . . " And for us to come to share that love and that holy passion with him seems to me the supreme miracle of the divine grace. The manufacture of worlds, the sowing broadcast of stars—these are little things in comparison to making a selfish man into an unselfish."

These people, having come to look on the world

through eyes that had seen the cross, had come to share Christ's own estimate of values. Jesus had vast experience in giving—none other ever gave with such mad abandon. "Ye know the grace of our Lord Jesus Christ," said Paul, "that, though he was rich, yet for your sakes he became poor, that ye through his poverty might be rich." He became so poor that he had to borrow a stable in which to be born. He became so poor that he had to borrow a donkey upon which to ride to his death. Having given thus recklessly, he could speak about giving with authority. And what conclusion did he reach? This, "It is more blessed to give than to receive." Receiving is a great privilege—we have all had vast experiences in that. We have been great receivers. But there is a richer privilege even than that. That is the privilege of *giving*. Such was the conviction of Jesus. Such was also the conviction of these saints who had come to share his nature.

Not only does Paul tell us that their changed attitude toward giving was born "of the grace of God," but he tells us further how God was able to work this mighty change within them. It is an old story, but it is the only story. He was enabled to bring about this amazing transformation through their own personal surrender. "First," he said, "they gave themselves to the Lord." When we do that, when we put ourselves wholeheartedly into his hands, we of necessity give him our substance as well. If we do less, our surrender is incomplete. I know it is possible for one to be liberal and yet not be Christian. But it is utterly impossible for one to be Christian and at the same time greedy, grasping, and selfish. These people, then, possessed a new attitude toward giving because they had been made new creatures in Christ Jesus.

III

Now look how this change affected their giving.

1. They gave voluntarily. Paul did not have to seek them and wring an unwilling donation from their hands; they sought him. There are two types of givers in the church. One is made up of those who give voluntarily, and the other is made up of those who have to be conscripted. These latter will give, but they must be sought and pressed and pushed into a corner. Of course, that is far better than not giving at all, but you will agree that it is only a second best.

The first car I ever owned was a Hupmobile. After driving it for some fifteen minutes, I decided that I was an expert. In this conviction, I drove into my garage, and straight on through it. While my car was being repaired, I had a call to the country. The garage man lent me his car; it was a self-starter—the first I had ever seen. On my way, I had to cross a creek with a mud bottom. In the middle of this creek, I killed my engine. I was distressed. How could a minister officiate at a wedding after wading about in mud knee-deep to crank his car? Then it occurred to me that it was a self-starter. How refreshing! We have saints like that too. But there are still others that we have to crank. God bless them both, but we especially thank him for the self-starters.

2. They gave cheerfully, eagerly; that is the kind of giving that appeals to the heart of our Lord. Paul tells us, "The Lord loveth a cheerful giver." There is nothing surprising about that—that is the kind we love. Who wants a gift that comes with a snarl? Thackeray, in his lecture on Swift, tells how the great Dean would spend himself in the services of others. But he adds this damning sentence, "He insulted you while he served you." We all know something of that type. Then he adds, "I had rather have had a potato and a kind word from Goldsmith than to have been beholden to the great Dean for a guinea and a dinner."

Though I have been married for a good many years now, on my return from a trip away from home, I still bring my wife a box of candy—sometimes. It is possible that she has come in some measure to expect such a gift. But suppose I should come in after one of those absences and fling the box at her with a growl and say, "There it is. I brought it, but I didn't want to. The only reason I did, was because I knew there would be a row if I didn't." I daresay she would not greatly appreciate it. I have known folks to give to the church so reluctantly, so snarlingly, that you felt, in the language of Thackeray, that they insulted the cause and the God back of the cause while they served. But these Macedonians were cheerful givers.

3. These people gave according to their ability. That is right and reasonable. The man with one talent is not expected to do as much as the one who has two or five. When Paul in another letter gave directions for giving, he put it on this basis, "Upon the first day of the week let every one of you lay by him in store as God hath prospered him." We should give according to our ability. That is, we should do our best. Where that is done, there is never any financial problem. But so often there are those who deny themselves the privilege of carrying their part of the load. A handful of pledge cards makes interesting reading. While there are some pledges that are so mean in proportion to ability that they depress us, there are others that are so beautiful that we feel like shouting for joy.

4. They gave sacrificially; that is the kind of giving that is priceless. "To their ability," Paul said, "Yea, and beyond their ability, they gave." The shadow of the cross fell athwart their checkbooks. Their giving was fragrant with the breath of Calvary. It is such giving that enriches. It blesses both him who gives and those who receive. It is this type of giving, and this only, that wins our Lord's highest approval. We never hear any praise from his lips for the prudent and conservative giver. He never becomes enthusiastic over the man who says, "I will do my part, provided the other fellow will do his." His praise is only for those who give with reckless abandon.

One day for instance, as he sat over against the

treasury, he watched the people as they made their offering. The story says that many that were rich cast in much. That was fine. But Jesus did not get excited over this giving. By and by a woman came wearing weeds of widowhood. She dropped in two mites— less than three mills, and a mill is the nearest nothing I have ever seen. Then Jesus sprang to his feet in glad enthusiasm. "This poor widow has cast more in," he declared, "than all they who have cast into the treasury." Who will be the largest giver in our church this year? The one whose gift has in it the largest measure of sacrificial love.

Now let me close with this question: What is your attitude toward giving? Is giving for you a pain, or is it a pleasure? is it a joy, or is it a sorrow? is it an opportunity to be embraced songfully, or a galling burden to be born in grief? This is one of the sharpest and most accurate tests of the vitality of our religion. If a call to share leaves us cold, the chances are vastly great that we have lost our way. But if we greet such calls with gladness, we may be reasonably sure that we have become partakers of the Divine Nature. For the right kind of giving is the most Godlike something that we can do. It is a sure way to become laborers together with him in the remaking of a world gone wrong. Therefore, wise and Christlike are these who join with the saints of the long ago in begging for the favor of being allowed to give.

XIII

WHAT HAPPENED AT PENTECOST

"What meaneth this?"

ACTS 2:12

PENTECOST IS THE GREATEST EVENT IN THE HISTORY of the Christian Church. But in spite of this, I am persuaded that for many earnest people it has little or no meaning. Some have become so mystified by that about it which is passing and non-essential that they have missed what is essential and abiding. Therefore, instead of fixing our minds upon the events of this story that we confessedly do not understand, let us think of that about it which we cannot help but understand. Let us forget for the moment the fiery tongues and the rushing wind and think of the change that this experience, whatever its nature, wrought in the disciples themselves. Having considered what this experience did for these friends of Jesus, we may be the better able to judge what that experience was.

I

What, then, did Pentecost do for the disciples themselves?

1. It welded them into a brotherhood. Any close reading of the Gospels will reveal the fact that one chief purpose of Jesus was to build a brotherhood. "By this," he said, "shall all men know that ye are my disciples, if ye have love one to another." He recognized that there were two types of personalities in the world —one made for hate, the other for love. One works toward the dividing of men, the other toward the uniting of them. He claimed that he himself was a uniting force. He claimed further that all who were engaged with him in the building of men into a brotherhood were his friends and that all others were his enemies. "He that is not with me is against me; and he that gathereth not with me scattereth abroad." His purpose, therefore, was the building of a brotherhood.

But in spite of the fact that Jesus gave his energies wholeheartedly to this high task, at the time of his death he seems to have made but little progress. He had gathered about him an inner circle of twelve men. But while these were outwardly one, inwardly they were far from being united. It is at once distressing and depressing to realize that they went into their last meal with their Master spitting hot words at each other as they wrangled over the old question as to who should be greatest in the kingdom. It was the Master himself who had to assume the role of a slave and wash his disciples' feet. Not one of them was brotherly enough to undertake this lowly task. But for Pentecost, this little organization would doubtless have melted like a rope of sand.

But after this experience in the Upper Room, Doctor Luke could say, "The multitude of them that believed were of one heart and of one soul." This oneness belonged to the original group that had been friends of Jesus before his crucifixion. Into it had been brought orthodox Jews of the homeland. Into it had also been brought foreign-born Jews from whom those of the homeland had been separated by a wide chasm. Into this brotherhood came a little later despised Samaritans and Gentiles. Thus men and women of different races and nationalities, of widely different social standing, were brought together in the bonds of a common brotherhood.

So close were these ties that those who had once been far apart worshiped and took communion together. Not only so, but at first they shared their material substance. "Neither said any of them that ought of the things that he possessed was his own; but they had all things common." This is the nearest approach to Christian communism that we find in the New Testament. It was a communism of spending, not of earning. As to detail it was imperfect. But the spirit that prompted it was an altogether right spirit. It was a spirit of brotherliness.

It was this devotion of one Christian to another, this

spirit of brotherliness, that was one of the most impressive characteristics of the early church. The pagan world looked on these little "colonies of heaven" with wistful wonder. "How these Christians love each other!" they said in amazement. And, because they wanted to love and be loved, they were drawn into these little groups. To this day there is nothing quite so impressive as a church that is a brotherhood. It is equally true that there is nothing that more grossly misrepresents our Lord than a church that is torn by strife and discord. Let the membership of any church get to fighting among themselves and the devil may take a holiday so far as that church is concerned. Pentecost welded the friends of Jesus into a brotherhood.

2. Then, through this experience these disciples became literally obsessed by a passion for witnessing. They had an irresistible urge to share their experience with their fellows. No sooner had the multitude come together, saying, "What meaneth this?" than Simon Peter was ready with an answer. He stood up with the eleven, Luke tells us. There was one spokesman, but every member of the group bore his testimony by standing up with the spokesman. One weakness of much of our modern witnessing is that so often the present-day Simon must stand up without the eleven. Those that should be there to back his testimony, to give it pungency and power, are not present. Simon Peter, with the backing of his fellow-saints, so testified

that men were cut to the heart, and and some three thousand were brought into the church.

A few days later Simon Peter, with John, is on his way to prayer meeting. At the gate of the temple, he is met by a professional beggar. This man asks for alms. Neither Peter nor John has any money, but they do have a passion to share their experience. Therefore, Simon preaches to this professional panhandler with the same hot enthusiasm that he has preached to the vast multitude. Not only so, but he preaches effectively. There is a new face at prayer meeting that day. This beggar is changed into a giver. He enters with Simon and John into the temple, "walking, and leaping, and praising God."

Other days have passed, and these two apostles have clashed with the authorities and are under arrest. These authorities are a bit at a loss to know what to do with them. But at last one offers this happy suggestion: "Let us straitly threaten them, that they speak henceforth to no man in this name." Therefore, they call Simon Peter and John and command them "not to speak at all nor teach in the name of Jesus." But Peter and John answer and say, "Whether it be right in the sight of God to hearken unto you more than unto God, judge ye. For we cannot but speak the things which we have seen and heard." Silence, they maintain, is for them an utter impossibility. They can no more cease from speaking than the grass can cease from growing green at the kiss of the springtime.

That these disciples were speaking only sober truth is evidenced by the rebuke of the authorities when they are again put under arrest. Listen to what they say. These authorities seem full of righteous indignation. "We commanded you not to teach nor to speak at all in the name of Jesus, and you have filled all Jerusalem with your teaching." How amazing! Among those that had heard the message were foreign-born Jews who were visiting in Jerusalem. One of them was a brilliant young chap by the name of Stephen. He at once came to be possessed by the same passion for telling his story. He witnessed with such power that his hearers, unable to resist his words with logic, resorted to stones. In fact, they dragged him outside the city and mobbed him.

Then what happened? It was now evident that to witness was dangerous. They could not do so except at the risk of personal danger. "Therefore," the story continues with strangest logic, "they that were scattered abroad went everywhere preaching the word." Thus, when these authorities sought to put out the holy fire that Pentecost had kindled, they failed utterly. Instead of putting it out, they only scattered it. Thus, by and by, the whole Roman world was set on fire. This was done, not by preaching from the pulpit, but by the testimony of nameless nobodies who laid almost violent hands on every chance passer-by to tell him of the amazing happenings that had taken place in their own lives and in those of their fellows. Pentecost gave to the friends of Jesus a passion for witnessing.

3. This experience also gave to the disciples an incredible joy and hopefulness and courage that fill us with wistful wonder to this hour. The very first impression they made upon outsiders was that theirs was the joy of the intoxicated. "They are full of new wine," was the easy explanation. Most of us know how a mild form of intoxication banishes the gloom, changes sadness into gladness, timidity into courage, and want into wealth. There is a classic Tennessee story of a poverty-stricken brother who met a friend that was on the point of moving to Texas. "I have a brother in Texas," he informed his friend. "I want you to tell him for me that my crops have failed, my hogs have died. Unless he helps me, I don't see how I can get through the winter." But a boon companion immensely cheered this impoverished man from his flask. Therefore, when he again met his friend an hour or so later, he merely said, "I have a brother in Texas. If you see him, tell him that if he needs anything just to let me know."

This absurd joyousness seems to have been born, at least in part, of the mad certainty of these disciples that they were sure to win. They believed that the kingdoms of this world were actually going to become the kingdoms of our Lord and of his Christ. In this mad faith, they faced stark impossibilities with holy laughter. They encountered the most deadly dangers unafraid. Opposed, arrested, publicly whipped, they knew neither discouragement nor resentment. They, rather, rejoiced that they were counted worthy to suffer shame for the sake of their victorious Lord. Thus, they lived in joyous expectancy. They were possessed by a boundless optimism and a dauntless courage that were all but irresistible.

4. Finally, this experience brought to these disciples amazing power. In fact, it enabled them to do what any sane man would have said was flatly impossible. Suppose one had said to a spectator who saw that little prayer-meeting crowd of one hundred twenty on the way to the Upper Room in the Temple, "There moves a group that is going to shake this entire city. They are going to shake the whole Jewish nation. They are going to shake the whole Roman world. Age-old abuses like infanticide and slavery are going to vanish before them. They are going to breathe on all the sub-sequent centuries like a spiritual springtime." Who would have believed it? "Impossible!" any sane man would have said. Yet, history declares that this actually did happen.

II

This, then, is the effect: a brotherly church, a church with a passion for witnessing, a church with a joyous optimism and a dauntless courage, a church with amazing power. What was the cause? How did this group of believers come to be this kind of church?

Suppose we listen to the testimony of those who were present and who participated in this great event. They explain the change that had been wrought in themselves in terms of the Divine. They use varied words to express this conviction, but it all adds up to this: they have not simply come upon new evidences of God or of the resurrection of Jesus; they have, rather, come to a new and compelling awareness of God himself. They have come to realize beyond a peradventure that the Christ who was crucified is really alive. Not only so, he is both with and within them, individually. He is also among them as a group. They know that in giving the Holy Spirit, God has given himself. Thus they tell us that the change that has been wrought in them has been wrought by God and God alone.

It is my conviction that their testimony is true. I believe this because no other explanation will satisfy. We simply cannot account for what these ordinary men and women became and what they did in any other way. Then, I believe that their explanation is correct because it really does explain. They became the kind of men and women, and did the kind of work, that I should expect God-possessed men and women to become and to do. After this experience they ceased painstakingly to imitate Christ and came spontaneously to reproduce him. They sing with St. Paul, "For me to live is Christ. . . . I am crucified with Christ: nevertheless, I live; yet not I, but Christ liveth in me." Should I say

"Tennyson liveth in me," you would expect me to sing in some fashion as Tennyson sang. These people, claiming to be indwelt of Christ, went out to live even as he lived.

Look, for instance, at this picture. Here is a man, brilliant, gifted, possessed by that love of life that belongs to young manhood at its best. Yet, this young man, Stephen by name, meets an untimely death. Because he dares to speak his deepest convictions, he is dragged without the city gates and cruelly mobbed. But he dies without bitterness, and there is a light upon his face that was never seen on land or sea. As he falls asleep, he prays this prayer: "Lord, lay not this sin to their charge." That marks him as a close kinsman to him, who, when hung on the cross, prayed thus for his enemies: "Father, forgive them; for they know not what they do." We cannot account for such lives except in terms of God.

Just as we cannot account for what these men became apart from God, no more can we account for what they accomplished. They were without social standing. They were without wealth. They did not have enough influence to avoid the whipping-post and the jail, the arena and the stake. Yet they turned the world upside down. But they never think of these mighty changes as wrought by themselves. "Do not look on us," Simon Peter warns, "as if by our own power or holiness we had done this. God has thus glorified his Servant Jesus." And always, when Paul reports the results of his missionary efforts, it is not what he and his fellows have accomplished, but what God has done through them. They could no more have accomplished what they did accomplish apart from his experience of God than a drop of water could change the Sahara Desert into a flower garden. This is the only explanation that really explains.

III

What, then, does Pentecost mean for us?

It means that this same transforming and empowering experience of God is for you and me. This is the testimony of Simon Peter as he spoke on that distant day: "The promise is unto you, and to your children, and to all that are afar off, even as many as the Lord our God shall call." This is to be the experience, not of the exceptional Christian, but of all Christians. It is an experience that is perfectly normal. Any other is subnormal. Nothing is more evident than that our Lord never intended that you and I should carry on in the energy of the flesh. Through our very failures, he is saying to us what he said in the long ago, "Apart from me, ye can do nothing." It is only in and through him that we can become and do our best.

It is, therefore, highly reasonable that the experience that made these early saints what they were should be available for us. Certainly there was never a greater need for a God who is able to do exceedingly abundantly above all that we can ask or think than there is today. Only God can enable us to save a civilization that threatens to collapse into an abysm of blood and tears through unbrotherly hate. If there is not a power that can remake us and equip us for the task of building the kingdom of God, then I see no hope for our world.

If, then, this experience is available for us, how can we enter upon it? How do we avail ourselves of that mighty power called electricity? We do so by discovering the laws of electricity and being obedient to them. It is thus that we avail ourselves of the power of God. "We are his witnesses of these things; and so is also the Holy Ghost whom God hath given to them that obey him." As the room is flooded with sunshine when the blinds are lifted, so our lives are flooded by his presence when we open the door for his incoming. He is not merchandise to be bought. He is a gift to be received. "Of his fullness have all we received."

On the farm where I spent my boyhood, under the deep shade of beech and oak trees there is a great flat rock. Upon the face of this rock, hands that have doubtless been dust for centuries once chiseled a basin. In spite of the fact that this basin is as lifeless as death, it sings and prattles with one of the most luxurious springs that a thirsty man ever kissed upon the lips. Go to this spring in the dead of winter or in the noontide hush of midsummer, and you will find it prattling and laughing like a happy child. How is it that this basin offers its life-giving cup to every passer-by through all the changing years? In answer to this question, the basin can only point to the majestic hill that towers in the background, and say, "Of its fullness have I received." It is such receiving that makes the finest of giving possible for ourselves. "If any man thirst, let him come unto me, and drink. He that believeth on me, as the scripture hath said, out of his inner life shall flow rivers of living water. (But this spake he of the Spirit, which they that believe on him should receive.)"

XIV

WHY DO WE SUFFER?

"Who did sin, this man, or his parents, that he was born blind?"

JOHN 9:2

HERE IS A MAN WHO HAS LIVED HIS ENTIRE LIFE IN the night, while others have been enjoying the daylight. He has been compelled to idle, while others have been privileged to work. He has been forced to be a parasite, while others have had an opportunity to do something in the service of others. These friends of Jesus rightly conclude that there is something wrong. They are sure that this was not God's original purpose for this man. Therefore, they ask this question: "Who did sin, this man, or his parents, that he was born blind?" Thus they sought an answer to about the most perplexing problem in all the world, the problem of suffering.

177

I

But to whom is suffering a problem?

It is certainly not a problem to the atheist. It is, of course, a fact with which he as well as the believer has to reckon. But it is not a problem. If you believe that man is "the product of blind forces that had no pre-vision of what they were creating," then evil with all its attendant suffering is the most natural thing in the world. Under such circumstances the one irrational thing would not be evil; it would be goodness. Assuming that we are creatures sprung from mud, the fact that we ever love well enough to serve and suffer for each other surely is a problem beyond the power of any man to solve.

Suffering, then, is a problem only for the believer. Since we believe that God is the Creator of all things, since we believe that he is Almighty, since we believe that his nature and his name is love; since we believe that he is perfect goodness, it is perplexing that this world that he has made should have in it so much of tragic suffering. No wonder that as men have suffered in body and in mind, no wonder that as they have been tortured by the sufferings of others, they have at times cried with the Master, "My God, my God, why?" For it does seem at times "as if some lesser god had made the world, and had not power to make it as he would." If God is like the Christ that gathered little children in his arms, if he is like the Man that went to the cross for you and me, how can there be so much of pain in a world that he created, and that he is supposed to rule? This, I repeat, is one of the most vexing problems with which we have to deal. How are we to explain it?

II

Do not think for a moment that I am so presumptuous as to believe that I can give a full answer to this riddle of the ages. Countless millions have thought upon it. They have been forced to think by the tragedy of their own lives, as well as by that of the lives of those about them. They have had to find some sort of answer. Let us look at some of these answers.

1. There is the answer of these disciples. It is evident that they share the faith of their people, and that in brief is this: All suffering is born directly of sin. Wherever, therefore, there is a sufferer, there is also a sinner. Suffering is proof positive of sin on the part of him who suffers. When Job was afflicted by his boils, and still more sorely, by his friends, the one question of these friends concerned, not the fact, but the nature of Job's sin. That he had sinned was not a matter for argument. That was already proven by his pathetic plight. He was suffering, wasn't he? Then, of course, he was guilty. "Whoever suffered being innocent?"

Well, millions have so suffered. Yet there is enough truth in this false faith to keep it alive. Some do suffer, as we shall see later, as the direct result of their own sin. But to say that all great sufferers are also great sinners is as utterly false as to affirm that all who manage to dodge suffering are great saints. Experience tears this easy faith into tatters. We have all known good men to go to the wall, while bad men prospered. Jesus does not give a full explanation of the suffering of this blind man. But he, at least, makes it plain that his suffering is not born of the sin either of his parents or of himself. The answer to the riddle of pain, therefore, must go deeper than to affirm that it is the direct result of sin on the part of the sufferer.

2. There are those who place the blame for their suffering upon fate. This is the case with a vast number. For centuries this has been the faith of the religions of India. It is also the faith of Islam. If suffering comes, it is not the natural result of an ordered world. It is not because men reap what they sow. It is all caused by fate. This ugly faith had a considerable revival among ourselves during the World War. There were many soldiers that believed that if a certain bullet had their name upon it, it would get them regardless. But if fate had not intended it for them, they were in no danger, however exposed.

We meet this faith again and again among our fellows. When I sought to warn a friend not to expose himself needlessly during a thunderstorm, he replied that if he were to be killed by a thunderstorm, he would be killed anyway. Hence, there was nothing for him to do about it. A few days ago one of our papers carried this amazing story: One morning a little girl in Florida told her mother of a bad dream of the night before. She dreamed that she had been run over by a car and killed. A few days later, by a strange co-incidence, her dream came true. What then? The parents of this girl charged her death to fate. The driver of the car was not arrested. Whether he was careless or drunk, we do not know. We only know that these parents thought that they themselves and their little girl were in the hands, not of God, but of blind fate.

Of course, you remind me that this is sheer paganism. Certainly. Yet some of the choicest of the saints have believed a doctrine closely akin to this. Take the Puritans, for instance. They believed in predestination. They believed that God had determined everything in advance. If a man made a right choice, it was because God willed it. If he made a wrong choice, it was for the same reason. Of course, this struck a death blow to human freedom. It meant that Judas was no more to blame for betraying the Master than was Paul for dying for him. Sadder still, it made God the author not only of all good, but also of all evil. Of course, from such a faith we must turn with utter horror.

3. Then, there were those who, realizing the unreasonableness of sin and suffering in a God-ordered world, sought to get rid of the problem by denying the reality of these evils. Men persisted in believing that they

really suffered, but this was due to what Spinoza called "darkness of the mind." Mrs. Eddy traced it later to an error of mortal mind. But assuming the rightness of their position, they did not thus get rid of suffering. They only gave it a new explanation. All the pain still remained. The faith healer of Deal, to whom another has called attention, makes this clear.

> "There was a faith healer of Deal
> Who said, 'Although pain is not real,
>   When I sit on a pin
>   And it punctures my skin,
> I do not like what I fancy I feel.' "

We cannot get rid of grim realities like sin and suffering by merely shutting our eyes.

4. Why, then, do we suffer? Let me say again that a complete answer to this question is impossible. Yet there are certain causes that are obvious to us all. While we Christians do not believe God to be author of evil, he does make evil with its resulting agonies a possibility. This he does by creating us as free agents. We are gifted with the power of choice. When we come to the forks of the road, we can turn either to the right or to the left. When a choice is to be made, we can take the road that leads toward the depths or the one that leads toward the heights. God had to give us this power or make us less than men.

Now, having the power of choice, some of us misuse that power by making wrong choices. Such wrong choices always bring suffering. This does not mean, of course, that everyone who suffers has made a wrong choice. We have already pointed out that Jesus made it plain that this blind man was not suffering either because of his own sin or that of his parents. It is true that there are some who suffer because they are reaping what they have sown. There are some who suffer because they are bad. But there are others who suffer because they are good. The only sinless Soul that ever touched this world died of sheer heartbreak in spite of his sinlessness.

But when we have faced the fact that there is suffering that is not the direct result of sin, it is only truth to say that most of the suffering of this world is born of sin either on the part of the individual or of the group. If as individuals and as groups we should make right choices, then much of the sickness of the mind as well as of the body would be avoided. Also, the suffering born of social injustice, and the far greater suffering born of war, would be over. Even many of those calamities that we are accustomed to call "acts of God" would be far less harmful. One has called attention to the fact that the larger part of the tragedy of the San Francisco earthquake was due to the shoddy mortar that had gone into the building of that ill-fated city. The wrong choices we make, therefore, count for much of the suffering that we face in our present world. It is the price we pay for our misuse of freedom.

We must realize, of course, that the fact that God makes suffering thus possible, does not mean that he is the direct author of our suffering. I knew a mother some time ago who gave her son a car. She intended for him to use that car to get to school. She intended also that the car should give her boy pleasure. But he did not use it according to her purpose. He drove it recklessly. Soon he wrecked it and came very near to wrecking himself. But nobody thought of arresting this mother. It was not her gift that all but killed her boy; it was rather his misuse of the gift. Even so, it is our misuse of God's gift of freedom that accounts for very much of our suffering.

Then some of our suffering is the price we pay for living in an ordered world. In one of McGuffey's readers there is the story of a chap who got hard hit in the battle of life. The wounds that he suffered so embittered him that he said desperately: "I wish I were in a world of chance." No sooner had he made this wish than he went to sleep to wake, as he wished, in a world of chance. Suddenly his tooth began to ache. He remembered the remedy that he had been accustomed to use in his ordered world; he would make hot coffee and hold it in his mouth. But now, when he put the coffee to boil, it froze. In the same fashion everything went wrong, till he wished himself once more in an ordered world. It strikes me that all of us would prefer that kind of world in spite of the fact that it calls us again and again to face grim tragedy.

How cruel, for instance, the law of gravitation can be! Yet without this heartless law we could not live on this planet. How horribly destructive is fire! The other day our papers carried the picture of a father and mother with faces bowed in their hands in grief. They had left their two children, ages one and five, asleep at home. The house caught fire, and they were burned to death. But we cannot blame God for this. Fire at its best is so friendly that the ancients believed it was stolen from heaven. But, being what it is, it must always burn, anywhere and in any age. If this were not the case, infinitely greater suffering would result because we could never know on what to depend. A part of our suffering, therefore, is the price we pay for living in an ordered world.

Finally, some of our suffering is the price we pay for belonging to one another. We are part of a family. Being thus closely tied up with others, "if one member suffers, all members suffer with it; if one member rejoices, all members rejoice." I have seen enough joy look out from a mother's eyes whose son has made good to raise the temperature of heaven. But she must pay for this high capacity for rejoicing in his joy by a like capacity to share in his shame and suffering. Much of suffering, therefore, is the price we pay for our misuse of freedom, for living in an ordered world, and for membership in a family.

III

What then is to be our attitude to suffering?

1. We are to expect it. This does not mean we are to seek it. This does not mean that we are not to avoid all needless suffering. But it does mean that facing the fact that we live in our kind of world, we cannot hope to avoid all struggle, all suffering, all pain. Ours is a world of conflict. Ours is a world where we accomplish nothing except at the price of effort. To expect to get our shins barked now and then, to expect more or less of pain and heartache, therefore, is only reasonable.

To speak in this fashion is not to use the language of pessimism, but of sound sense. If my boy were going in for football for the first time, I should deem it the part, at once, of wisdom and of kindness to tell him something of what to expect. "Those eleven men that are opposing your team," I should say, "are not going to deal altogether gently with you. They are going to give you some hard knocks. You must look for some jarring falls. But in spite of all this, it is a thrilling game; and I want you to play it, and to play it your best." So Jesus spoke to his friends, "In the world ye shall have tribulation: but be of good cheer; I have overcome the world."

2. Accept it. Paul in his letter to Timothy calls on this timid young man to accept his share of the hardships. "Of course, we accept it," you answer cynically. "We cannot do otherwise." But we can. There are

some who surrender to suffering, who give over the fight, and who spend their days in self-pitying invalidism. There are those who grow harsh and bitter and resentful on account of their suffering. These do not accept it. They only submit in weakness, or with stealthy rage, to their hard lot.

We should accept suffering because it is a badge of greatness. As creatures rise in the scale of being, that rise may be measured by their capacity for pain. One crab can make his dinner off a lesser crab, while a yet larger one is making his dinner off of the middle-sized crab. Yet they are so low in the scale of being that there is too little pain for them to know that they are being devoured. I dread pain terribly. But I do not care to buy exemption from it by becoming a crab. I shall try to hearten myself by remembering that great suffering is possible only to a great creature.

Then great suffering may be a great trust. If you have been called upon greatly to suffer, it may mean that you have been given a post of signal difficulty that carries with it signal honor. Not only may such a post be one of signal honor, but of great reinforcements as well. Since God's grace is always sufficient, he comes especially near to those whose lot it is to suffer. Accept your suffering, then, as a badge of superiority, and also as an honor, in that you are called to serve at a difficult post.

3. Use your suffering. While capacity for pain is a mark of greatness, pain in itself is not necessarily

good. It may be an unspeakable evil. But it is always possible to make suffering into good. There are certain types of pain, for instance, that serve to warn us. A headache is not a disease; it is a symptom. It is a red flag that nature waves before our eyes to tell us that we are on the wrong road. But for my capacity for physical pain, I might drop my hand upon a red hot stove some morning and never know that I had burned it off till I undertook to tie my shoe. Just as physical pain may warn me that I am on the wrong road, so also may the pain of a hungry heart or of an outraged conscience.

Not only is pain a warning signal, it may be a means of growth. If God had been seeking our comfort above everything else, he might have contrived to make this a less painful world. But he is out after character, not comfort. Therefore, he makes a world where it is possible for us to have a very hard time. But this may be vastly helpful. A soft summer breeze may be better to sleep under, but we need the cruel whips of tempest to lash us into our best. This is the reason that those who have suffered are usually the ones who are at once most strong and most tender. This is especially true of those who allow their suffering to bring them closer to God.

Do you remember Gwen's Canyon in Ralph Connor's *Sky Pilot?* Gwen was a lovely and willful creature, with a temper as inflammable as gunpowder. One day as she was riding in the round-up, her horse stepped into a prairie-dog hole and fell. She failed to fall clear of her horse, was caught under him, and so badly injured that she could never walk nor ride again. It was so strange and horrible to this willful creature that she rebelled. For days and weeks she lay in her father's cabin raging in bitter agony at her fate.

Then, one day the Sky Pilot dared to make her visit. He rode down through the canyon that she loved, and up to her cabin. "Did it hurt," he said, "when they put the plaster cast on you?"

"You bet," she said. "It was awful."

"What a pity," he replied, "that your father was not here. He would not have allowed the doctors to hurt you like that."

"Oh," she answered. "But he was here. He wanted them to do it. You see they put the plaster cast on me to help me sit up a little and maybe to walk sometime."

"Oh," said the Pilot, "then they did not hurt you just for the fun of the thing?" He then told her the story of the canyon.

"Once," he said, "there was no canyon but only a wide-stretching prairie. On day the lord of the prairie walked out over it. He enjoyed its beauties, but he missed the flowers that he loved the best. He then sent the winds and the birds to sow the seed of those flowers. But no sooner had the flowers sprung up than they withered. At last in seeming anger he sent a thunderbolt that cleft the prairie to its heart. For a long time it groaned from its black wound. But, by and by, a brook sprang up in the depths of the canyon and flowers began to bloom, and a cool sweet place it was, with all its sights, and sounds, and silences. It became the place that the lord of the prairie loved the best. And the fruits of the Spirit," continued the Pilot, "are love, and joy, and peace. And some of these grow at their best only in the canyon." [1]

Paul found this to be true in his own experience. After he had learned much through suffering, he declared, "We know that to them that love God all things work together for good." You may not understand why you suffer the particular heartache that is now yours. Well, you do not have to understand, you only have to believe. If, in spite of your lack of understanding, you remain within the will of God, you, too, will discover that, regardless of the nature of suffering, it may be made to work for your good. You will come to thank God, not only for those experiences that seemed to enrich, but for those also that seemed to promise nothing but utter poverty.

"O Joy that seekest me through pain,
    I cannot close my heart to Thee.
I trace the rainbow through the rain,
And feel the promise is not vain,
    That morn shall tearless be."

---

[1] Used by permission of Fleming H. Revell Co., publishers.

XV

THE MAN WITH A PREJUDICE

"Can there any good thing come out of Nazareth?"

JOHN 1:46

I

WE KNOW VERY LITTLE AS TO WHAT NATHANAEL said. We know still less of what he did. But we do know what he was. That is by far the most important. What does this brief passage tell us about him?

1. He was a man of deep and genuine honesty. We sometimes speak of common honesty as if it were a virtue that is quite as plentiful as blackberries, but as a matter of fact downright honesty is not common at all. It is about as rare as it is beautiful. When Jesus saw Nathanael coming to him, he said, "Behold an Israelite indeed, in whom is no guile!—Here," he seems to say, " is a princely man without one single flaw of insincerity or deceit."

The word takes us back to that scene by the brook, where Jacob had his transforming experience. Shrewd and self-sufficient Jacob, after years of successful rascality, is on his way to claim his inheritance. But on the borderland he is stopped. "There wrestled a man with him until the breaking of the day."

"What is thy name?" is the question of his Antagonist, who is also his truest Friend.

"Jacob," is the reluctant answer. "I am a trickster, a fraud. I have lived by my wits. I am as slippery as an eel."

"Thy name shall be called no more Jacob," comes the response, "but Israel; for as a prince hast thou power with God and with men, and hast prevailed." Nathanael is an Israelite after this high fashion.

It is evident that Jesus greeted this man with genuine appreciation. There is no vice that our Lord seems to have hated with greater intensity than hypocrisy. He hated this evil because the hypocrite injures others. But the deadliest blow that the hypocrite strikes is at himself. A man may deceive his brother of set purpose and thereby do that brother genuine harm. But his hypocrisy reaches its climax of evil when he no longer recognizes it as hypocrisy. The Pharisee who prayed thus with himself, "God, I thank thee, that I am not as other men," is all the more hopeless because he has come to believe in his own sincerity. He has lied to himself until he has come to believe his own lie. That is insincerity at its worst.

Just as Jesus hated hypocrisy with supreme intensity, so he loved sincerity with equal intensity. He recognized the fact that sincerity is a fundamental virtue. It is the foundation without which no substantial structure can be built. Carlyle reminds us that if we build a lie into a rock wall, it will fall down. The same is true if we build a lie into a character. Sincerity is the fountain out of which flow the beautiful streams of frankness, honesty, simplicity. Naturally, therefore, Jesus welcomed the man about whom he could say, "Behold an Israelite indeed, in whom is no guile!"

2. Not only was Nathanael genuinely sincere, but he was devoutly religious. He was a man of prayer. He was evidently one of those choice souls who was standing upon his watchtower in an evil hour, scanning the horizon in expectation of the dawning of a better day. There were a few men and women of this type even in that dark day. Simeon, you remember, was one. Being expectant, he saw the Deliverer even in a little child. Therefore, he took Mary's baby into his arms and said, "Lord, now lettest thou thy servant depart in peace, for mine eyes have seen thy salvation." Anna also was one of those who was living in expectation of a Deliverer.

It is this expectancy that was a predominant characteristic of the great prophets. That which made them prophets was the fact that they were living in daily expectation of some notable intervention on the part of God. They were constantly saying, "Look out!

In a world like ours, God-made and God-ruled, something wonderful is likely to happen at any moment." And their expectation of great things from God made it possible for God to do great things. Expectant souls always give God an opportunity. These are they that become channels through which his transforming power may flow to a needy world.

Expectation was a special characteristic of the early Church. There was a word that was constantly upon their lips; that was "Maranatha." There was so much in this word that the translators did not put it into English. Maranatha, the Lord is coming! It was a greeting among the early Christians. At other times it was a password. When they met in their secret meetings, all one had to say to be admitted was "Maranatha." It was upon their lips as they went forth on their missionary journeys. It made them radiant, songful, unspeakably courageous. At any moment their victorious Lord might break in upon them.

We have lost that expectation in large measure. One reason for this is that these early saints were mistaken as to the method of our Lord's coming. They, as some today, expected a physical coming of Jesus. That they were wrong, the centuries have demonstrated. But that many of us have given up the expectation of the physical return of Jesus does not mean that we should give up the expectation of his return in any fashion. The coming of Jesus is spiritual and progressive. Constantly he is waiting to break in upon us with some new light and some new victory. But our hearts have grown dull and our eyes have lost their luster because we have lost our expectation.

Maranatha! What does this word mean to us? It ought to help us to face with poise and courage the big impossibilities that confront us today. How do you feel about the future of the Church? Is it to be a dwindling power or is there yet stirring in your soul a mad conviction that it is to be a glorious church without spot or blemish or any such thing? How do you feel about international relationships? Have the nations grown too mad ever to be sane again? Is civilization to collapse in unbrotherly conflict, or will men yet beat their swords into plowshares and their spears into pruninghooks and learn war no more? Never did we need the attitude of these early saints more than we need it today. They faced grim impossibilities and conquered because they were made strong by an invincible expectation.

3. But along with these fine virtues, Nathanael had one defect. It was such a glaring and positive defect that it came very near to cheating him out of his dearest hopes and of his finest possibilities. He had read his Bible. He knew the expectations of his people. He was doubtless looking for the Messiah. Therefore, it was a grand moment when Philip dashed in upon him and said with hot enthusiasm, "We have found him, of whom Moses in the law, and the prophets, did write, Jesus of Nazareth." That was the greatest news

he had ever heard. But there was one word in the message that was so jarring that it threw all the music of Philip's sermon into discord. Nathanael had doubtless known men from Nazareth who were rascals. Some of them perchance had cheated him. Therefore, he had come to have a prejudice against Nazareth. So intense was this prejudice that he came very near to rejecting Jesus altogether, because he did not like the town from whence he came.

II

Now when we come to talk about this man with a prejudice, we are also talking about ourselves. We all have our prejudices. Of course, mine are not so bad as yours for the simple reason that they are mine. I also realize very readily that from your point of view mine are rather narrow-minded and contemptible, whereas yours are the prejudices that naturally occur to those who are broad-minded and intelligent. But regardless of the nature of our prejudices, the chances are that all of us possess at least one or two and with some they are quite numerous.

Nor am I going to make a wholesale condemnation of all prejudices. While a prejudice is a conclusion which we reach without adequate reason, yet a first-class prejudice may prove of value. I was brought up in an old-fashioned home where liquor was not allowed for any reason. There was instilled into me a deep-seated prejudice against any alcoholic beverage. My antipathy was not based altogether on reason. If you had asked me why I was so grimly opposed to liquor, I might not have been able to give an intelligent answer. You might have dismissed me by saying, "You are prejudiced." Even so, that prejudice has stood me in good stead more than once.

For instance, when as a boy of fifteen, I paid my first visit to the city, I fell in with a crowd from my own community. This happened to be a drinking crowd. I went with them because the situation was to me so new and strange. Little by little, as they began to get intoxicated, they insisted upon my drinking; but I refused. I refused even when the pressure got so heavy as to involve bodily danger. My resistance was born largely of prejudice, I confess; but it was a wholesome prejudice. Therefore, I remember it with pride rather than with shame.

Then there are prejudices because of which I have favored certain objects or institutions. I have reasons for valuing these institutions, but that does not mean that I am not prejudiced in their favor. Take the Church for instance. Some folks delight in criticising the Church. They love to find every possible fault. But as for myself I am a churchman. I am prejudiced in its favor. I am not so blind as not to recognize its faults. But when there is a question regarding the Church, I do not claim that I bring to it an altogether unbiased mind. I am prejudiced in favor of the

Church, as I am of monogamous marriage and the Christian home.

But while prejudice may be an asset, as a rule it is a liability. It has a tendency so to stop our ears and to blind our eyes that we refuse to face the facts. Some years ago, I taught school in a community that was dominated by a very aggressive group of what we called Non-progressive Campbellites. These were equally violent in their political beliefs. They were all Democrats. But there was one rather staunch family that was Methodist and Republican. One day the head of this Republican-Methodist clan made this rather startling declaration: "I am a Republican and a Methodist, and I would continue to be both if I knew I was wrong." That has in it an element of prejudice.

Some time ago a young woman came to see me to tell me why, in spite of her own needs and needs of her friends and of her world, she had persisted in rejecting Christ. She told me how, as a young girl, she had known a certain minister who won a large place in her confidence. By and by that minister proved himself, not a genuine disciple of Christ, but a rather disgraceful crook. This had given her a prejudice against all ministers, all churches, against Jesus Christ himself.

While I was a student at Harvard University, I knew a young man who was an avowed atheist; but in spite of this fact we were very close friends. He had many fine qualities. In most respects, he was broad-minded and honest; but, because of the circumstances of his early childhood, he was deeply prejudiced against religion. One day I turned with him to the end of the Gospel of John, where it reads, "These are written, that ye might believe that Jesus is the Christ, the Son of God; and that believing ye might have life through his name." "Will you," I said, "take this book and examine the evidence as you would concerning any other matter?" He refused, not from reason, but from prejudice.

That is a significant story we read in the twenty-second chapter of Acts. Paul has been arrested by certain fanatics. Roman soldiers have had to take a hand to keep him from being torn limb from limb. When they bring him to the palace, he asks permission to speak to the crowd. When his request is granted, he begins tactfully, speaking to them in Hebrew. He tells them how he has been brought up in Jerusalem at the feet of Gamaliel. He also tells them how he once persecuted the Church. This is all to their liking; therefore, they listen with rapt attention. But at last he ventures to tell them how God sent him to speak to the Gentiles. At once there is an explosion. They break into an uproar and refuse to hear another word; that is, they listen till the speaker touches the tender nerve of their prejudice. Then they refuse to hear him any more.

Thus does prejudice stop our ears and blind our eyes again and again. What had Nathanael to say against Jesus? Only this: "I have known some bad people from Nazareth; therefore, I won't believe in anybody that comes from that town." We feel the same about whole nations. Hitler-ruled Germany is a Jew-hating nation; therefore, every German must hate the Jews. Japan is raping China; therefore, every Japanese must be a blood-thirsty militarist. Thus we reach our conclusions through prejudice rather than through honest reasoning. Thus we injure others, but we inflict the sharpest wounds upon ourselves. Nathanael was a man with a perjudice, even as you and I.

III

Now what did Philip have to say to this highly prejudiced man? Well, he did not give him a piece of his mind. He did not tell him how narrow and pig-headed he was. Perhaps that is the course we should have taken. We are sometimes fond of showing people their own pictures that we ourselves have drawn. But such a course seldom gets either them or ourselves very far on the road. A prejudiced man may be very annoying, but we are not likely to help him by verbally shaking our fists in his face.

What then, I repeat, did Philip do? He took the only sane course open to him. He did not argue as to whether Nazareth was good or bad, decent or indecent. He did not even argue about Jesus. He virtually said, "You are in doubt as to whether Jesus is the Messiah because of the place from whence he comes. I cannot prove to you that he is, just as you cannot prove that he is not. But if you are honest in your doubt, you can find out for yourself. If you really wish to know the truth, come and see." In thus inviting, he pointed the only way really to know anything that is worth knowing; that is, by experience.

When our second boy was a little chap, he used to have an irritating question that he would ask about every dish that was new to him. When his mother would urge him to eat, he would hold off and say, "How does it taste?" Of course, no one could give a satisfactory answer to that question. How does spinach taste? Very much like nothing! Yet, I confess, that that is not a fully adequate description of spinach. How does it feel to fall in love? No one can tell. How does it feel to hold your first-born in your arms? Again, no one can tell. How does it feel to have your heart broken? You can know only from experience.

Nathanael decided to try the matter out. As he was coming, Jesus paid him this fine compliment: "Behold, an Israelite indeed!" Nathanael was amazed. He felt himself understood. "Here is a man," he said, "that knows me just as I am." And he responded by saying, "Thou art the Christ." Jesus said, "You shall see greater things than these." And I make bold to say no man has ever taken Nathanael's road and been disappointed. Therefore, I dare to challenge you with this appeal, "Come and see!" He will not fail you.

This is the clear and explicit promise of Jesus himself. "If any man will do his will, he shall know."

A few years ago, I went to deal with a rather clever young agnostic who lived near my church. I spent a whole evening with him. He was well informed, and enjoyed arguing. Therefore, we talked much without getting anywhere. When I left him, I had a depressing conviction that I had all but wasted both my time and his. But my visit accomplished at least this much, that he came out to hear me preach.

At this service, I appealed to him to "come and see." In response he came forward and united with the church. When the service was over, some of his friends gathered round to congratulate him, but he was a bit embarrassed. When they were gone, he came to me alone and said, "Don't misunderstand me. I am a stranger to Jesus Christ, but you said that, if I would surrender to him, I would find him. I have done that."

"All right," I replied, "that is all Jesus himself requires. Leave the rest with him."

His wife told me the remainder of the story. When they got home from church, he said, "Ina, can you pray?"

"Not much," she said, "but I am willing to do my best."

"Let us kneel together and pray." Ina began, but she prayed only a few words until her husband broke in, took the prayer away from her, and finished it himself. The next time I saw him he had come to spiritual certainity. The questions that had perplexed him yesterday bothered him no more than the fact that Jesus came from Nazareth bothered Nathanael after he had come to know Jesus himself. Therefore, I bring to your heart, as to mine, anew this invitation: "Come and see."

XVI

THE VICTORY

"The victory is ours, thank God!"

I CORINTHIANS 15:57 (MOFFATT)

HERE IS A WORD THAT THRILLS WITH THE DEATH-
less joys of Easter. It speaks home to our deepest longings, and to our highest and holiest hopes. It is
a word to make us stand up and cheer. The man who
gladdens us with this heartening declaration has the victory of which he speaks looking out from his own eyes
and ringing in his own voice. He looks upon hard-pres-
sed men and women, like ourselves, who are but shattered fragment of broken families, and who are hurrying
on to what looks like final defeat, and shouts "We have
won. It is ours to set our feet upon the neck of our
foe and bound with joy and gladness. The victory is
ours, thank God!"

THE VICTORY

I

What is this victory that makes Paul so joyful?

There are victories that are so temporary and trifling that to win them is of little consequence. They do not last. Often they fail to satisfy, even for the brief moment that they are ours. Then there are victories that mean something to a very few, but to the many they mean nothing at all.

For instance, a few days ago our newspapers carried the name of a young chap who had been the most intimate friend of my son while we were living in Birmingham. This deserving young fellow, who is as poor as a church mouse, had entered a movie contest. He had written some fifty words on why he liked "You Can't Take It With You." By so doing, he won a prize of ten thousand dollars. The victory was his. Of course, it brought him great gladness. His friends also naturally rejoiced with him. But these were comparatively few. To the many his victory simply meant nothing at all. But this victory over which Paul is shouting means something to all of us.

Then there are victories that have in them more of tragedy than of triumph. In James Barrie's little play, "The Will," you remember the lovely young couple that visited their attorney one day in London. The young husband was beginning to prosper, and his wife was eager that he make a will. She was bent on his leaving a part of his small fortune to certain charities in which they were both interested. Then he had two sweet old maiden aunts that were dependent on him. These, too, must be provided for. Both husband and wife were so beautifully unselfish in their attitude that the gloomy office of the solicitor seemed to take on a new radiance. When they were gone, the lawyer felt as if springtime had paid him a visit.

Ten years slip by and this husband and wife are again in the lawyer's office. The husband has continued to prosper during these ten years. He is now far richer than he used to be. In consequence, his wife has become more vain and self-centered. She has also gained in avoirdupois till today she seems not so much dressed as upholstered. This time she has come with a different purpose from the one that first brought her. To use her own words she has come to see that her husband does not do anything foolish. By this she means that she has come to see that her husband does not give a penny of his money away. Nothing is to be left to the orphanage—it would only encourage the children to grow up useless. Nothing is to be left to the old aunts—they are parasites anyway. When the couple have gone this time, the solicitor feels as if he has been nipped by a killing frost.

Other years slip by, and there is a final scene. The husband is again in the office of his solicitor, this time alone. He is far richer now than ever. Everything that he has touched has turned to gold. But there is no tenderness in his face, and no gladness looks out from his tired eyes. He glares at his solicitor, and spits out these tragic words: "My wife is dead, my son is a rotter, my daughter has run away with the chauffeur. Take this paper, it has the names of the men with whom I have sought most furiously for gold. Leave my money to them with my respectful curses." In the eyes of the world this man had won. The victory was his. But it was a victory that was shot through with tragic defeat.

Almost a quarter of a century ago the Allies won a war. What a shout of joy went up with the signing of the Armistice! "The victory is ours," we cried, "thank God!" But what an unsatisfactory victory it has proved to be! We see now that it had in it far more of sorrow than of joy, more of war than of peace, more of death than of life. This the case with so many of our victories. Comparatively few of us win. But, even when we do, our victories are generally defective. Some are so because they concern only the few. Many of them are unsatisfactory because they are so fleeting, or have in them the seeds of defeat. But the victory over which Paul shouts is for all of us, and it abides for all time and for all eternity.

What, then, I repeat, is this victory? It is an all-inclusive victory. It includes the conquest of every foe that we are called upon to face. But the foe of which Paul is thinking especially is that most vindictive and victorious of all foes, which we call death. Paul claims that victory over death is ours. Surely this is a matter of vital interest to all of us. This is true for one reason, at least, and that is because death is an experience through which all of us must pass. This is the case regardless of what may be our attitude toward death. Our attitudes are quite varied.

Some of us, for instance, because we fear death, seek to ignore it. We try to get rid of this unwelcome adventure by refusing to think of it. Some time ago a little chap stood in front of me, tightly closed his eyes, and said, "You can't see me." But the fact that he had shut his eyes did not put mine out. I could see him in spite of his deliberate blindness. So it is with death. We cannot get rid of this grim fact, or any other, by simply refusing to face it. The message of Easter therefore concerns us all because all of us must pass through the experience of death.

Then there are others who try to treat death, and what lies beyond, with entire indifference. "One world at a time," they say with a shrug. "It does not matter to me in the least whether the grave ends all or whether it does not." This attitude may be possible for some of us for a little while. It may be possible as we think simply of our own dying. But it is not possible when we think of the passing of those we love. However you may feel about your own going, you cannot see your mother pass into the valley of the shadow and say, "It doesn't matter to me in the least whether she has become a clod, or whether she is consciously alive in the Father's house." You cannot say such a heartless word as you hold your own baby in your arms. Believe me, there comes a time to all of us when about the biggest question in the world is this age-old question, "If a man die, shall he live again?"

Paul is here affirming that death is not a terminus but a thoroughfare, not a blind alley but a gateway. We are going to continue to live after the experience of death. This is the case whether we desire to do so or whether we do not. In a conversation with a friend some time ago, he justified himself for a bit of conduct that he did not think quite ethical by saying, "But a man must live."

"Certainly," I answered. "A man must live. But if by that you mean he must live a certain number of days, months, or years, here, about that I do not know, and neither do you. But somewhere, out beyond the experience of death and the grave, a man must live."

But Paul means far more in his assertion of victory than that we shall merely continue to live. The victory that thrills Paul is not the thought of continued existence, but of continued right existence. It is only this kind of victory over death that makes everlasting life worth while. Merely to exist is not enough. Tens of thousands fling out of life in the here and now. They find the life that now is so intolerable that they cannot stand to see it through till the whistle blows. Unless, therefore, there is a quality of life richer than the one they now possess, it would only be direst tragedy for it to continue into the eternities. But when Paul shouts "The victory is ours," he means not simply that eternal existence is ours, but eternal right existence. This is the only victory that would not have in it more of sorrow than of joy.

II

Upon what does Paul base his conviction of victory? We may be sure that he has some reason for the faith that is in him. Paul is not a mere credulous dullard. He is one of the gigantic intellects of the centuries. Why, then, does he claim the victory?

1. One reason for his making this claim is that he believes in the resurrection of Jesus. As to his reasons for so believing, it is not my purpose to speak now. But that he did so believe, no one can deny. The resurrection of Jesus is central in Paul's preaching, as it is in the preaching of his fellow Christians of that day. When he sums up his gospel, he does so in these words: "I delivered unto you first of all that which I also received, how that Christ died for our sins according to the scriptures; and that he was buried, and that he rose again the third day according to the scriptures." Even assuming that Paul does not claim that the resurrection of Jesus is proof positive that we shall rise, he certainly is convinced that the fact of his resurrection makes our own rising a strong and reasonable hope.

2. Then, I think Paul believes in victory over death because he believes in the supreme worth of human personality. He believes that the universe is rational. He cannot, therefore, conclude that a reasonable God

will throw away the one superlative value that he has created. Personality is the one thing in this world that is of real value. When Jesus put the most chaffy personality in one pan of the scales and the world in the other, the world shot up as if it were a mere bit of thistle-down. Would it not be a strange thing if a maker of fine vases were to work at his task with no saner purpose than to dash the work of his hands to pieces at the close of the day? Paul is sure that this world is not a mere madhouse, presided over by a mad God. He is sure that it is rational. Therefore he believes that the victory is ours.

3. Paul believes in victory over death because he is keen enough to realize that we are living in the unseen in the here and now. We have a silly saying, "Seeing is believing." But if we believe only in what we see, then we do not believe in any of those forces and values that are supreme. We do not believe in the law of gravitation, for not one of us has seen it. We do not even believe in faith or in love. I asked a company of small boys and girls the other day, "What is love?" They sat in utter silence, just exactly as you would if I were to ask you the same question. But not one of you would for that reason deny the existence of love. All our lives are conditioned in the here and now upon the unseen.

But you say, "I have seen people die and pass into the unseen, but I have never seen any of them come back." True, but did you see them before they went?

In speaking of your friend, you say, "He has a beautiful personality." No doubt, but did you ever see that personality? Not once. You have never seen me, and I have never seen you. Of course I have seen the house in which you live, and you have seen the house in which I live. But that is all. If you lose a finger, you have not lost the slightest bit of your personality. The same is true if you lose an arm or a limb. In fact, some of you have thrown away more than a half dozen bodies, but you are still the same personalities you were before. Therefore, if you can continue to be yourself while you throw your body away on the installment plan, it is reasonable to believe that you will go on being yourself after you throw it away in a lump sum at the close of the day.

4. But Paul's supreme reason for claiming victory is a present experience. Not only is he living now in the presence and power of the unseen, but he is living victoriously. In the fellowship of his risen Lord he is finding life a daily triumph. Of course, if life is for you a present defeat, it will not be so easy for you to believe in future victory. Sometimes we try to persuade ourselves that we can lie down in moral failure and wake up victorious. But such a faith has no encouragement in the New Testament. If God cannot give us victory here, we cannot be very sure that he can give it to us anywhere. How futile to expect the undertaker, or the coffin, to do for us what our victorious Lord has failed to do. But since Paul is living

now in the realization of victory, it is only reasonable to expect that that victory, won through Christ, will go on forever. Therefore he joyfully asks, "Who shall separate us from the love of Christ?" Then he brushes all foes aside as so many flimsy nothings as he shouts, "I am persuaded, that neither death nor life, ... nor any other creature, shall be able to separate us from the love of God, which is in Christ Jesus our Lord." Walking with the stride of a conqueror today, he believes that he will go on conquering forever.

III

What is to be the practical effect of this high faith? Suppose we should be able to join in Paul's glad shout, "The victory is ours!" what would it do for us? I am sure it would do for us something of what it did for him. What, then, did this high faith do for Paul?

1. It put a song of gratitude in his heart that absolutely nothing could hush. We find this valiant saint in all sorts of trying situations. At times, he is being stoned, whipped, imprisoned. We find him at times seemingly forsaken of God and man. But we never find him without his song of gratitude. That song here rises to thrilling heights as he sings "The victory is ours, thank God!"

2. This faith made Paul a tireless worker. It ought to do the same for us. "Be ye steadfast, unmovable, always abounding in the work of the Lord, forasmuch as ye know that your labor is not in vain in the Lord.—

Here," he claims, "is a place where you may invest with the assurance that your investment will never go for nothing." That ought to quicken our interest. We know what it is to suffer loss. Some of us have trusted the wrong bank. We have put our money in the wrong enterprise. But here we cannot lose. Jesus tells us that the man who gives so much as a cup of cold water in his name makes an investment for eternity. We are to work, therefore, in the assurance that those for whom we work are creatures of eternity, and that what we do for them is as abiding as God.

3. Then this fact enabled Paul to face the future— both the near future and the far future—not only with calm confidence, but with eager expectancy. A lad of fifteen, who used to attend our services, faced the fact recently that he must go early through the experience of death. There always seems something especially tragic in the passing of those who are yet in life's green spring. But this lad had been greatly blessed by having a wise and consecrated mother. Therefore he was able to face this new experience somewhat as he might have faced his first ocean voyage or his first flight in an airship. "I do not mind," he said; "there are so many things that I want to know." So it was with Paul. He looked upon his entrance into the other life as his finest and gladdest adventure.

IV

How may this victory become ours? The Apostle

is in no doubt as to the answer to this question. We do not win by sheer force or by grim determination. This victory is a gift. It is a gift of God through Christ. That ought not to surprise us. How did physical life become ours? Not through our own efforts. There was a mother that went down into the valley of the shadow of death for us. Our life was a physical gift from her, and primarily a gift from God. And so it is with eternal life. "Thanks be to God, which giveth us the victory through our Lord Jesus Christ."

How, then, do we get hold upon this life that means victory in the here and now, and victory forever? We do it by getting hold on God through Christ. And this we do by trusting him enough to put our lives in his keeping. "He that hath the Son hath life.—He that heareth my word, and believeth on him that sent me, hath everlasting life.—This is life eternal, that they might know thee the only true God, and Jesus Christ, whom thou hast sent." To possess Christ, therefore, and to be possessed by him, is to have a present victory. It is also to have a victory that will last forever more. To be able to say, "I know whom I have believed," is to possess a quality of life over which death has no power.

This is far more than mere theory. So far as my experience goes, I have yet to find one living in the consciousness of God who was not sure of life both here and yonder. Years ago, I watched my father pass "to where beyond these voices there is peace." He had a good voice. He used to lead the singing in our village church. As the end drew near, he stretched out those once strong hands, that were very weak now, and sang, "Jesus, Lover of my soul, let me to thy bosom fly." He was joyously confident that the Everlasting Arms, upon which he was leaning as he pushed his tired feet into the waters of death, would sustain him through those waters, and on into the eternal yonder. Sure of God's sufficiency in the here and now, he was sure that he would prove sufficient for evermore. This is also our faith. Therefore, we join our voices with that of Saint Paul, and shout "The victory is ours, thank God!"